WRITING
ESSAYS
ABOUT
LITERATURE

WRITING ESSAYS ABOUT LITERATURE

*A Brief Guide for University
and College Students*

SECOND EDITION

Katherine O. Acheson

BROADVIEW PRESS

BROADVIEW PRESS – www.broadviewpress.com
Peterborough, Ontario, Canada

Founded in 1985, Broadview Press remains a wholly independent publishing house. Broadview's focus is on academic publishing; our titles are accessible to university and college students as well as scholars and general readers. With 800 titles in print, Broadview has become a leading international publisher in the humanities, with worldwide distribution. Broadview is committed to environmentally responsible publishing and fair business practices.

LIBRARY AND ARCHIVES CANADA CATALOGUING IN PUBLICATION

Title: Writing essays about literature : a brief guide for university and college students / Katherine O. Acheson.
Names: Acheson, Katherine O., 1963- author.
Description: Second edition. | Includes bibliographical references and index.
Identifiers: Canadiana (print) 20200393804 | Canadiana (ebook) 2020039391X | ISBN 9781554815517 (softcover) | ISBN 9781770487987 (PDF) | ISBN 9781460407479 (EPUB)
Subjects: LCSH: Academic writing—Textbooks. | LCSH: Report writing—Textbooks. | LCSH: Essay— Authorship—Textbooks. | LCSH: English language—Rhetoric— Textbooks.
Classification: LCC LB2369 .A24 2021 | DDC 808.02—dc23

Broadview Press handles its own distribution in North America:
PO Box 1243, Peterborough, Ontario K9J 7H5, Canada
555 Riverwalk Parkway, Tonawanda, NY 14150, USA
Tel: (705) 743-8990; Fax: (705) 743-8353
email: customerservice@broadviewpress.com

For all territories outside of North America, distribution is handled by Eurospan Group.

Canada

Broadview Press acknowledges the financial support of the Government of Canada for our publishing activities.

Edited by Martin R. Boyne
Book design by Michel Vrana

PRINTED IN CANADA

For Mary Osler, Katherine Stevens, and Gladys Guest,
who taught me most of what I know about words.

Contents

Section One

INTRODUCTION

CHAPTER ONE

The Purpose of an Essay about Literature

THERE ARE TWO QUESTIONS INSTRUCTORS IN LITERARY studies dread hearing from students. The first is "did we do anything important in the class that I missed?" This is what we call a loaded question: I have to agree to premises that put me in a position I don't want to be in. An example of a loaded question is "Do you always burn the toast?" To answer this, I need to agree that I have been burning the toast. To answer the question about what was missed in class, I have to accept the possibility that nothing important happened (or that something did but I'm too cranky to repeat it for the student). The instructor perceives this question as a challenge to their talent or to the inherent interest of the course's subject matter. But I understand, when I get this question, that the student is asking if the missed class presented something that they need to know to do well on the graded components of the course, so I usually mention those and then ask the student to find a classmate who is willing to share their notes.

The other question is "what do you want in this essay?" This question is more complicated. It's loaded too, though: it implies that there is an ideal essay tucked away in my head, and a clever student can get a glimpse of it if I let down my guard or if I like the student personally enough to give special attention to them. There's a whole bunch that's whacky about that set of implications. One, there is no ideal essay. Two, if there were, I wouldn't have it hidden away in the darker recesses of my brain; I'd have it out on the table for everyone to see. Three, my desires, whims, or even ideas, and the extent to which your essay reflects them, are not what the assignment is about. So the answers I give to this question are always a bit kooky: I say, "I want to be enlightened and moved" or "I want to make no corrections to pronoun agreement" or "I want to discover the secret of eternal life" or "I want to finish grading before the end of the holidays, or at least soon thereafter." Or I can be more helpful and say that I want a clearly written argument, based on evidence, about the meaning, power, or structure of the work or works the essay discusses. Yes, let's repeat that—*a clearly written argument, based on evidence, about the meaning, power, or structure of the work or works.* That's what teachers really want.

In my courses, I'm quite careful about letting students know what I want and how to accomplish it. Grading is one of the most valuable things I do for students, and I would hate for them to think that I don't have objective and measurable reasons for evaluating their work in the way that I do, that there is no rational process to assessing an essay. I give them a breakdown of what's important for written assignments and what the weighting of each category is. And I'll go over in class how to get from beginning to end in the essay-writing process and how to write the best possible essay. There is a method to writing a good essay, and there are clear and manageable steps to take from start to finish. That's what this book is about. For those of you who already know how to write great essays, I'm sorry to have to take the mystery out of the process; you know the secrets, and I'm going to blurt them out here. It's about sharing, and that's good. And we can all learn something new, however proficient we already are. We all want to have AHA! moments, and writing a great essay will give you more than one.

LITERATURE: INSTRUCTION, DELIGHT, IMITATION

Literature is as complex as an ecosystem, as ineffable as the sub-atomic world, as rich and beautiful and interesting as the many cultures around us. It is shaped by the world, and it shapes our understanding of the world. It is made from language, an infinitely malleable and sinuous medium. It can be found in the simplest, most naïve forms and the most carefully crafted; its authors can be children with few skills or geniuses who have worked for years to hone their art. Literature in English is read all around the world and has been central to advanced education for hundreds of years. Literature is powerfully ideological; it can be subversive, oppressive, or any combination of the two. Literature comforts us, frightens us, brings us to tears, creates bonds, and opens up possibilities for our imaginations. The reasons we study literature—the reasons we write essays about literature—are to try to understand better what it gives us, how it reflects, enlarges, and critiques what it is to be human in this world, or these worlds, of ours.

Literature's principal purposes are different from those of other systems, and those differences shape how we approach it. From classical times until the present, literary critics have been in agreement about what literature does. The first thing that literature does, we believe, is to *instruct* its readers. Instruction can come in many forms, and a huge range of information, values, and ideas is conveyed in works of literature. The author may intend us to learn certain things, but we can also learn things that the author or authors didn't plan on us knowing. Those things can be about the society that the work depicts—that it is prejudiced toward women, for example, or that its religious values permeate all of the things that happen in it. They can be about the ideas that are represented in the work: we might perceive that the scientific ideas of the protagonist are related to their ideas about art, related in a way that the author didn't consciously intend us to perceive. They can be about the material world in which the story is set: we can make connections, as readers, between certain objects and ideas, between things and feelings, that also help us to understand more about the world, the characters, and the action that is represented in the work.

It may be important to you to distinguish between intended and unintended effects: it's always interesting, for instance, to read what an author says they were trying to do in a work and measure that against what you think actually got done. But because the medium of literature is language, because readers are individuals in particular cultural and social situations, and because works of literature are read in different times and places, much of the effect of a work of literature is out of the control of the author. These are reasons we keep going back to the same texts: they are never quite the same. And the enduring freshness of literary masterpieces also means we have endlessly interesting questions about what complex works of literature *mean*, which is why we keep on writing essays!

The second purpose of literature, we agree, is to *delight* its audience. Delight means to cause pleasure, so the effect is emotional. But the emotions that give us pleasure are not just joyful ones: we can take pleasure from sadness, for example, or from terror. Why else would we pay to see tear-jerkers and horror movies? One of the things we value most in art and entertainment is intensity of emotion; as a species, we like a good cry, a rush of adrenalin, a belly laugh, a shiver of fear. Psychologists and neuroscientists may be able to tell us why; perhaps rehearsing emotions that help us take action or communicate needs is just as important as staying in good physical shape. Perhaps reading literature, watching plays and films, and listening to music are as essential to our well-being as vitamins and minerals. But what we as students of literature focus on is what the emotions are, how they are produced by literary works, and how they are related to other things in works of literature and in the worlds in which they were produced and are read. As with their plan to instruct readers, authors may intend us to have certain emotions, but their works may produce emotions that are well in excess of their plans, or opposite to their intentions. These are all fair game for literary critics—of whom, I think I forgot to tell you, you are one.

The third purpose of literature is to *imitate life*, to produce for the reader a believable version of a world that is or that could be. This might be an internal world (the thoughts and feelings of one being, usually a person, but sometimes an animal or even an object), or it might be the world of a set of people in a culture or of a whole society. It might be a real world that has existed or does exist, it might be a fantastical world inhabited by outlandish creatures with magical powers, or it might be an ideal and imaginary world in which perfectly beautiful beings possessing the essence of being-ness float effortlessly above the drossy world we inhabit. Literary critics are interested in how authors build worlds and in how readers experience these worlds. We are interested in the opportunities and limitations that different kinds of worlds offer to the kinds of ideas and feelings that can be produced within them. For instance, science fiction can offer a different understanding of the human body and a different experience of its capabilities than can an eighteenth-century realist novel set in a small village in England.

But we are also interested in how authors make worlds out of language. If you think about this art, it's like making a house out of ice or a dress out of sand or a dessert out of cauliflower—there's magic involved in taking symbols, scribbles on a page, and turning them into something colorful, believable, sensuous, vibrant, and captivating. Much of what literary critics do involves examining the craft of literary construction: Why does this word work better than others? What is the effect of this way of representing thought or conversation? Why does this point of view make the emotional content more powerful? Literary critics are experts in how literature is made—in how the choices authors make and the experiences readers bring to works produce the rich, beautiful, and varied worlds that inhabit the pages of the books we read.

THE LITERARY ESSAY

Evidence

A couple of pages ago, I said that the task of a student assigned to write an essay about literature is to present *a clearly written argument, based on evidence, about the meaning, power, or structure of the work or works*. The previous section has given us a bit more detail about literature and about why we are interested in the meaning (the "instruction"), the power (the "delight"), and the construction of the work or works (how it "imitates" the world it represents). The rest of this book will be about the other terms in that sentence: how to collect and use evidence and how to write a clear and cogent argument from that evidence. But let me say a few things about those two right now, by way of introduction.

Literary studies is an evidence-based discipline, just like science, law, or medicine. If you are a doctor, your patients will list their symptoms to you, and you will try to pull those together into a plausible explanation that identifies a cause for the effects they feel. If you were a police detective, called to the scene of a crime, you would collect clues—a stray hair, a bloody knife, a used glass—and then try to put those and other bits of information together in order to produce a story that explains the body, the robbery, and the mysterious symbols painted on the mirror. The symptoms and clues you are analyzing, as a literary critic, are the ideas and feelings produced by the work of literature and the things that are used to make it—the words. From this evidence, you will produce a narrative that offers an explanation for the effects the work of literature has.

If you think of yourself as a detective or a doctor and you examine the work of literature and its context for clues, you too can diagnose the patient or solve the crime. I'll repeat myself: the study of literature is based on evidence, and its findings are arguments built from that evidence. The arguments must account for all the relevant evidence—there's no extra gun floating around, no additional ache or pain that's not explained by the illness you've decided on. That's how we know it's an adequate diagnosis of the illness or solution to the crime. Equally, all the evidence used to support the argument is necessary to the argument and is the best possible evidence that can be brought to the argument.

A large part of the assessment of your essay will depend on the quality of the evidence you collect, and another portion of the assessment of your essay will depend on how well you construct the explanation from it. These features are more important than the actual topic that you go after. Sometimes, at least in my experience, students think that I'm looking for them to find a certain meaning in a work or experience a particular feeling—that doing these things is key to unlocking the mysterious ideal essay I'm supposedly keeping safe and secret in my brain. But that's not what I value in a student's essay, or in an essay by a colleague or peer: I'm looking for well-gathered evidence pulled together in a compelling and convincing argument. Even if the essay topic is set for you, the value of what you have to say about the topic will depend on the power of the clues you gather and the persuasiveness of the argument you make out of them. Because of the importance of evidence and argument in literary studies, much of this book is devoted to how to conduct research in and about the literary works that you read and how to build an argument from that evidence.

Communication

Clear writing is a challenge for us all. It's a challenge for me, and, as an English professor, I'm basically a part-time professional writer, so sometimes I feel like it shouldn't be as hard as it can be! But essay writing doesn't need to be frightening or even difficult; there are methods to the development of clear writing, and we will look more closely at those in later parts of this book. It should help to know that literary essays are about concrete evidence: once you have the evidence assembled and have organized it into the building blocks of the argument you want to offer, all you have to do is tell the story of the evidence. It may also help to remember that you are writing about your evidence and your argument. Your argument is about the work of literature, but one important thing to avoid in writing about literature is plot summary: do not forget that you must tell the story of your argument in your essay, not the story of the work you are writing about.

The key to clear writing is to write clearly. How's that for clarity? Not very good: that sentence ends where it begins and begins again where it ends. But the point is this: there is no secret fix for effective writing. Writing is about words and putting them together. If you want to write clearly, you have to choose the words that mean what you want to say. Choosing words that you think might mean what you want to say is not good enough. You may want to use a dictionary to make sure that the words you are using mean what you want them to mean. If you think of yourself as a doctor or a detective, you'll realize that precise vocabulary is essential to getting your point across, explaining how you've diagnosed the disease or solved the crime. We could also compare essay writing to other kinds of writing. For instance, if you are writing an instructional manual for how to assemble a piece of furniture ...

Students also tell me that reading literature and writing essays are both subjective. By this I think they mean that, if I judge what they are saying in an essay or how they read and write about literature, I am in some way imposing an assessment on their personalities, their likes and dislikes, their feelings and inclinations. I would never want to do that, and I hope that I never have done it. But I'd like to clarify here the ways in which reading and writing about literature are subjective and the ways in which they are not. I think it will help you to write your essays and to understand the assessment process.

There are two meanings of "subjective" that are relevant here. The first is the one we've been using above. "Subjective," in this sense, describes something that is based on personal opinions or feelings and not on verifiable external facts. If I were to give you a bad grade on an essay because I didn't like the way you dressed or because I thought that you didn't like me (you never laugh at my fantastic jokes!) or because I'm cranky and mean-spirited (especially on weekdays), then I would be being "subjective" and—I think—incompetent as a teacher. If you were to write an essay that said unsubstantiated but *feeling* things about a novel that you just didn't like because it didn't have any romance in it or you didn't understand the language or you were upset about something in your real life outside of literature, you would be writing subjectively. As a teacher, I'd have to say you were really not doing your job as a literature student: the detective can't let his dislike of violence turn him away from the crime scene, and the doctor can't let her pain and sadness prevent her from telling patients the truth. Your feelings and opinions that are not grounded in evidence from the works you are studying do not have a place in your essay. In this respect, essay writing is not subjective but objective.

But, in another way, reading and writing about literature are certainly subjective. One of the most dynamic qualities of literature is that it means different things to different people. Each person's experience, knowledge, and interests are unique to that individual. One of the most fascinating areas of literary study is the analysis of reception through history—people didn't always idolize Shakespeare, for instance. And even when they did admire his works, they adapted them to the ideologies, tastes, and interests of their times. Our experiences of literature are similar: we bring what we are to the works. You are an individual subject. When you read a work of literature and talk and think and write about it, you bring your experience, knowledge, and interests to meet the material you are studying. This conjunction is one of the most powerful experiences we can have, and most of us remember one book or another as *formative*: it changed our lives. Your essays are about the experience of being you, reading the works you've read, describing the thoughts that you've had as a result.

Your perspective is an invaluable and essential part of the essays that you write. The essays you write will be accounts of what you have seen, thought, and felt *as a result of the literature that you have read* and about which you are writing. The ideas, perceptions, and feelings that you will convey in your essay are rooted not just in you but in your encounter with the work of literature. So you can show your reader where and why and how you had the idea, perception, or feeling you did, in the text (the evidence). And you can analyze your reactions to the text and show that analysis to your reader (the argument). In producing evidence for your feelings, insights, and thoughts from the text and in constructing an argument, you are able to share those feelings, insights, and thoughts with your reader. You know very well that if you tell someone what your feeling is—sadness or happiness or frustration—they can't feel it. They need you to tell them why you feel that way; they need examples, experiences, observations before they can empathize. It's the same in an essay: you have to point to evidence, explain your feelings in words, share your ideas, and persuade your reader to share your point of view. In this sense, writing essays is all about subjectivity—or rather about subjectivities. It's about sharing your subjective experience with other subjects, helping them see what you see, think what you think, and then, possibly, feel what you feel.

As a person, I am also an individual subject, with particular desires, preferences, and ways of dealing with the world around me. But I've had lots of experience as a teacher (even the newest teacher has had decades of education and years of practice). What I bring to the classroom, and what I bring to grading, is my "teacher-subjectivity." If I'm a good teacher, I've revealed to you in the course what my desires, preferences, and ways of dealing with things are as a teacher. I've told you what the learning objectives for the course are, I've given you some arguments that I think are persuasive about the texts we are studying, and I've adjusted those, or strengthened them, in response to your comments and questions. I've given you a detailed outline of what I want in an essay and shown you the relative importance of each component: I've told you that the quality of your argument will be worth more or less than other aspects, that how you handle evidence, how you write sentences, and how you document your sources will be worth a certain proportion of your grade. These preferences are the result of my years of teaching experience, of my objectives as a teacher, and of my interaction with students over the years. So yes, it's subjective, grading—I am a human being, and I bring to the texts we read and the essays I grade a set of inclinations that are unique to me. But a good teacher will have explained to you what they want, and why, and will have shown you much of how their teacher-subjectivity works in lectures and discussions. And a good teacher will always be willing to explain your grade, based on the evidence of your essay and the criteria he or she has put forward. Finally, a good teacher will always be willing to make an adjustment to your grade based on persuasive evidence that they have misjudged your work.

Our subjective experience as human beings is the great topic of literature, from the beginning of writing to the present. Sharing that experience subject to subject is what writing essays is all about. But sharing means communicating: it means finding the words for the feelings you have, reinventing the experience of your insight for your audience, and using logic to persuade your reader that yours is a valuable, meaningful, and interesting point of view. In this sense, writing essays is a template for the most profound of human experiences: communicating with another engaged and articulate person what you find moving, valuable, interesting, clever, brilliant, transcendent, joyful, tragic, enlightening. We might say that our goal as literary critics is to treat our subjectivity, and that of others, objectively—to study what it is to be human, to have language, to share with others. This is why we read, and it's why we write. We can learn to read more carefully, write more clearly, and communicate more strongly an objective view of the complex subjective interactions that make literature what it is.

HOW TO USE THIS BOOK

This book is designed to help you write the best essays you can write. It is my firm belief that every student who is a competent reader and writer can write an A-level essay. The best way to make sure that happens is to work from evidence to argument. If you follow the model described in the following chapters, you will need to take many notes from the works you are focusing on in your essay, and you will need to keep a list of ideas that come to you as you do your reading. You will also have to reread both the text you are working on and the notes you make from it. But, by the end of the evidence-gathering process (by the end of Chapter Five), you will have everything you need to write a first-class essay. The remainder of the book will help you arrange and connect your evidence so as to craft a persuasive, even beautiful, argument.

REVIEW QUESTIONS

1. What do teachers want in an essay?
2. What does literature do for people?
3. Why is a doctor or a detective a good metaphor for a literary scholar?
4. What are the most important qualities of writing for an essay about literature?
5. How is literary analysis subjective? How is it not subjective?

Section Two

RESEARCH AND ANALYSIS

CHAPTER TWO

Research within the Text

IF THE DISCIPLINE OF LITERARY STUDIES IS EVIDENCE BASED, where do we find the evidence? How do we know it when we see it? How do we keep track of it? This chapter will outline how to collect evidence from the first and most important source you have for your essay: the work you are writing about. (You could be writing an essay about more than one work, but, for this chapter, we'll just say "work.") All literary criticism, however far afield it ranges, starts and finishes with the literary text about which it is concerned.

For the purposes of this and the next three chapters, I'm pretending I've been assigned a four- to six-page essay (1,200–1,800 words) on a poem of my choice from the works I've studied in my imaginary literature course. I've chosen a short poem by William Carlos Williams. It's quite commonly anthologized, and you might have read it before. But reading it again won't take long. (One of the things to get used to in literary studies is not just reading but rereading. We always reread, and short works such as this can be reread many times.)

This Is Just To Say
William Carlos Williams

I have eaten
the plums
that were in
the icebox

and which   5
you were probably
saving
for breakfast.

Forgive me
they were delicious   10
so sweet
and so cold.

(By William Carlos Williams from The Collected Poems: Volume I, 1909–1939, copyright ©1938 by New Directions Publishing Corp. Reprinted by permission of New Directions Publishing Corp.)

TAKING NOTES ABOUT LITERATURE

In this chapter, we will discuss how to guide your reading of works of literature so as to help you produce evidence on which to base an essay. I recommend that you make careful notes about your responses and make a record of the parts of the text that inspired your response. I know that this will take time, but, I promise you, it will be time well spent. Date your notes, give headings such as the questions we will use below, and copy out quotations from the text (making sure to note the pages and line numbers accurately). This material—the combination of your responses and the basis for them—will be the foundation of your essay.

It takes time to write essays. If you don't keep track of the evidence you collect now, you'll have to go back and find it later. There are few things more frustrating than searching for a line or a sentence you know you've read but can't remember where. It's like looking for your keys or your glasses; you know they're in the house or your room, you know you saw them somewhere, but, for the life of you, you can't remember where. Taking the time to keep good notes from your reading will save you time later. Actually, writing things down helps fix them in your mind and makes your subsequent consideration of the evidence more fruitful. So take notes, either by hand or using your computer or phone, and keep them handy. Careful attention, close reading, and detailed notes will pay off when it comes time to write your essay.

You can take notes however you like. It helps to have them in a form that lets you easily find something and that you can easily rearrange. I tend to keep my notes in files on the computer. When I take notes, I make sure that the heading of the file includes all the bibliographic information I'll need if I use the notes in an essay. I am careful to take down as much of the quotation as could possibly be useful, knowing that I am not certain, as yet, how I will use it or how much of it will be useful. And I make sure to include the page or line number in parentheses after every quotation, even if there are a few in sequence from the same page. That way, if I cut or copy notes to somewhere else, I will retain the information that I need to document them. Finally, and I think most importantly, I label notes with key words that will help me locate them and organize them again.

RECORDING YOUR RESPONSES TO THE TEXT

Do I Like the Work?

Your first impressions of a work of literature are valuable starting points for your analysis of the work. Let's begin with a simple question: "Do you like it?" You probably do like "This Is Just To Say"; it's so short and sweet, delicious even. It's easier to write an essay about a work that you like, not just because the work will be more pleasant but also because the critical task is immediately clear: you can analyze why you like it. That analysis could well create the basis for your essay. If you don't like the work ... well, you can try to read it again, knowing that lots of people have liked it for quite a while. If that fails, you can figure out what you don't like about it. Whatever your level of affection for the work, this first feeling can really help you get started on collecting evidence. So make a quick note about your very first feelings about the work, and label it with the date or a title such as "first impressions" to remind you that these could be your opening thoughts toward an essay, a presentation, or an exam or test question.

GUIDING QUESTIONS

These questions can help you organize your response to a work of literature. Keeping track of these responses will give you valuable evidence to use in your essay.

- *Do I like the work?*
- *What words stand out?*
- *What feelings does it give me?*
- *Do I identify with any of the people represented?*
- *Is there anything about how it's written that stands out?*
- *What is the work about?*
- *What else is the work about?*

What Words Stand Out?

Our next question is about the vocabulary of the poem. Literature is built with words. When you read literature, you should be conscious of the fact that the author chose each word carefully, just as a painter chooses a color. For most of the works you will study, you can assume that the author has chosen words successfully: each word, and no other, best conveys their meaning exactly, works best with the other words in the text, and has associations or connections to other words that add to the meaning, power, or construction of the work.

When Hamlet asks whether it is "nobler" to suffer through life's pains and troubles than to commit suicide, he means *nobler*, not better or higher or braver or smarter. If you look up "noble" in a dictionary, you'll see why Shakespeare chose that word and what the consequences are to the sense of the passage and to our understanding of Hamlet's character. "Noble" suggests he is talking not just about what's best for a human to do but also about what's most fitting to his station as a prince, what's most praiseworthy in the eyes of secular and spiritual powers higher than he is. These meanings remind us that he is a very elevated person with special responsibilities in his society and that he answers to authorities that are both earthly and heavenly. The other words that might fit in the line don't convey those additional meanings.

At this point in your reading, you just want to make note of the words that strike you as especially important to the work you are studying. You don't need to think too much right now about why you select the words that you do—that's for a later phase of our work. In fact, you want to make note of words whether you think there's any reason for taking note of them or not—trust your instincts. Think of yourself as a detective or scientist: you need to open your mind, suspend your preconceptions, and collect anything and everything that's of interest. If you decide beforehand what you're looking for, you are guaranteed to miss some important pieces of evidence.

In "This Is Just To Say," you might have noticed "plums," "delicious," "sweet," and "cold." What a great set of words; if they were foods (and they aren't, even "plums"—they are words), we'd say they have terrific flavor, powerful scent, and fantastic mouth-feel (a great phrase that chefs use to describe the combination of texture and flavor that can make the experience of eating all the more enjoyable). You might also have noticed the word "icebox," which may be unfamiliar to you and gives a sense of when the poem was written and its setting. Another key word is "forgive," which is suggestive of the emotional tenor of the poem and the nature of its communication. Flag these words in the text and any others that you think are interesting. For example, "I" and "you" are very common words and unlikely to reward a dictionary search, but they are key words in this poem because they contribute distinctively to how the poem works. They emphasize that the poem is an act of communication between two people, so they are key to how the poem works and what it is about. List the words and their line numbers in your notes.

USE A DICTIONARY

Words are the building blocks of literature. Use an online or paperback dictionary to look up words that you haven't heard before or can't define for yourself. In the next chapter, we'll talk about how to use larger dictionaries as research resources.

What Feelings Does It Give Me?

The next question we are going to ask ourselves is what kind of feelings the work invokes in us. For me, there are four kinds of feelings that I have in response to "This Is Just To Say." One is sensual pleasure because of how evocative the poem is about eating plums, especially ones that come right out of the fridge. The poem vividly reminds me of that experience, which I have also had: the blueness or redness of the plums (though in my mind they are blue), the slight dusting of silver on their surface, the resistance of the skin as I bite through the plum, the too-cold feeling of its flesh, the sweetness of the juice, the hardness of the pit, and my manipulation of the fruit as I eat around it. The memory is sensual, in that it involves my senses, and pleasant; it may stimulate my appetite and have me moving toward the fridge. It's that strong!

The second is the feeling that is conveyed by the speaker's apology and their request for forgiveness: it's an awareness of the potential for moral or psychological reflection. The exact nature of this feeling will depend on the reader. Whatever your reaction, because the feelings associated with transgression and remorse are associated so closely with the rich sensual experience of eating the plums, both are intensified. Myself, I feel more naughty than bad, and I'm confident that forgiveness will be forthcoming for the speaker, so I don't feel much remorse or grief—a little, but not a lot. But that's me—you may have a more fully developed conscience!

Third, I have a feeling of witnessing an act of intimate communication between two people who love each other: I feel a little as if I am eavesdropping. This sensation is quite like the feeling that eating the plum is naughty; both feelings result from doing something that is irresistible yet perhaps wrong, something for which I feel remorse but not quite enough to stop me doing it again. The words that make me feel like an eavesdropper include "icebox" and "breakfast"; it's as if I'm looking into someone's kitchen at a time of day when guests are unusual or usually unwelcome. You may have different feelings—perhaps you feel part of the relationship, as if the note is written to you, because that accords with your experience and memories the best.

The fourth feeling is one that I often have when I read poetry. I don't know if you'll have this feeling. It might be the result of my training, experience, and profession. I'd be interested to know what feelings you have that are related to your own history! What I often feel when I read great works of literature—especially a poem such as this one, which is so short yet so moving and interesting—is awe and wonder: I'm amazed that anyone can take words and craft them into such a vivid, affective, beautiful, provocative expression. It's like making stained glass out of sand, growing a tree from a seed, or building a sonata from the keys of a piano: it's an amazing permutation of everyday things into something unique, beautiful, and powerful. This feeling isn't based on a set of words I can extract from the poem but rather on the whole, on how it has made me feel the other feelings I have had and on my vision of the imaginary world of the poem and of the people who inhabit it—all this accomplished in the space of 28 words!

In my notes, I'll write down a few sentences or phrases about each of these, and I'll try to attach the feelings to parts of the poem. My notes might say "sensual experience" and quote the lines that have given me that feeling; "remorse?" and the words that relate to that feeling; "intimate communication" and the evidence for that from the poem; and "beautiful" and a summary of my reasons for feeling that way. As you can see, the notes you take will help you reflect on why you have the feelings you do, and they will provide you with support for your analysis of those feelings. Those notes, that is, are the bridge between your reading and your essay, so I'll repeat: take the time to make them.

LITERATURE AND FEELINGS

Your feelings are personal, and you don't have to share them. But thinking about the feelings that literature provokes can lead to insights about the literature. Feelings can lead to thoughts, and thoughts are what essays are about.

Do I Identify with Any of the People Represented?

How many people are represented in this poem? Let's start with two: the speaker and the person to whom they are speaking. These are conventions of poetry; a poem is considered to have a "speaker," and that speaker is speaking to someone, if only to themselves. The speaker in this poem is the one who has eaten the plums, enjoyed them, and is, in the present of the poem, asking for forgiveness from the other person. Do you identify with the speaker? The second person in the poem is the person to whom the speaker's words are addressed. This person is the spouse or housemate of the speaker. Can you imagine yourself in their position? It's an interesting exercise: Do you feel that person is long-suffering or part of the fun? Do you think she or he really cares about the plums? Are they touched by the note, amused by it, or annoyed by the actions it describes?

Your identification with one or the other person in this poem depends partly on who you are and partly on how the writer has created each person. Examining the poem for the reasons that you identify with one or the other of the poem's characters will show you more about how the poem works. One of the great mysteries studied by literary scholars is how authors create believable characters out of words, people who appear to have thoughts, feelings, interactions, ideas, impulses, and conflicts—just like real people. Yet, more so than real people, they encourage us to learn about ourselves, our lives, and human beings and their worlds.

There are more people implied by the poem than just the characters it represents. There is, for example, the person we imagine to have written the poem. The speaker is a spontaneous, loving, mischievous, or even naughty person who, when scribbling the note that begins "This Is Just To Say," probably had plum juice dribbling down their chin. William Carlos Williams, I am quite certain, was not dribbling plum juice when he wrote this poem; he produced the poem after some reflection, and he may have edited it later for publication, even if he experienced the raw material for the poem firsthand. Even though the form of address in "This Is Just To Say" is so direct and unmediated that we imagine the author's self is pretty close in being to the speaker's self, we know that they are not identical. We can refer to the person we imagine writing the poem as its "implied author." And we can identify with that person: we can imagine having that experience and trying to turn it into a poem. We can imagine selecting the words, placing them in relation to each other, polishing it up. Again, this identification can give us insight into ourselves; it can also help us to look at the poem from the writerly perspective, as an illusion of a human interaction created by the artful arrangement of words.

Finally, poems and stories have implied readers, and plays have implied spectators. Occupying that role means being conscious of your role as reader in creating the meaning of the poem. In "This Is Just To Say," the fact that we seem to be overhearing (or over-reading?) an intimate, playful, emotional communication between two people is produced because we are positioned by the poem in a certain way. Even if we had no intention of eavesdropping—even if we'd be uncomfortable doing so in real life—we can't help but realize that we have done so by the time we've finished reading the poem! Our experience of the position of the implied reader also helps us to appreciate the construction of the poem, and may lead us to think about what the author wanted us to get out of it: we may realize, for instance, that much of what we learn about how relationships work, and how communication happens and why, is from reading, watching, and listening—rather than through direct experience. In this, as in so many ways, literature has a valuable lesson for us.

IDENTIFICATION

There are many reasons we identify with people, in real life and in literature. We feel that we share something with them and, therefore, can see a little bit from their point of view. We can be surprised by which characters we identify with and why: often we identify outside the boundaries of things we think are basic to our self-definition, such as our gender, our religion, or our cultural background.

Is There Anything about How It's Written That Stands Out?

The next question on our list is about technique. Sometimes we think of technique as the specialized use of resources that belong to a discipline, for which we have a whole vocabulary. You've heard some of the words that we use to talk about poetry: alliteration, allusion, enjambment, for instance. Alliteration means the repetition of consonant sounds; allusion means the reference to another work of literature; enjambment means separating the components of a grammatical unit with a line break, which can produce ambiguity or irony. But we don't care about things with fancy names at this point. What we want to notice in our first impressions is anything about how the writing is done that influences what we think is going on, what the poem means or makes us feel.

In "This Is Just To Say," the poem is written in the form of a communication from one person to another, in the style of a note that is left on a kitchen table or stuck on the fridge. These features reinforce our perception that the poem is part of the ongoing interaction between two people in a close relationship; exploring them can help us understand how the poem is built and, therefore, how it achieves its effects and meanings. The first thing we probably take note of, when we think of how "This Is Just To Say" is built, is that it doesn't really seem like a poem to us: the note on the kitchen table is *not a poem*. This is interesting: a poem that is trying to sound like *not a poem*!

In my list of first impressions, I'll write down the features of the poem that make me think that it is like ordinary, everyday communication—and not what we usually think of as a *poem*. First, "This Is Just To Say" has a very basic vocabulary and doesn't refer to literature or philosophy or theology, just to everyday things and events: "icebox," "breakfast," and "plums" are not rarefied or esoteric words. While I'm thinking about this, I might also note that there are certain kinds of words that are not part of "This Is Just To Say." There are no words of more than three syllables, for instance, and only two words that have three syllables; it is not written for an educated audience that might be thought to have a wide-ranging vocabulary and education in what students like to call "flowery" language. There are other features of the vocabulary that are interesting: for example, the poem uses the definite article "the" rather than the indefinite article "a/an," even though we are able to elide (or omit) the definite article with a plural noun. Saying "*the* plums" and "*the* icebox" instead of "plums" and "an icebox" points to a specific material reality, showing that the poem is more about things than it is about abstractions.

The sentence structures and grammatical choices are also interesting. The first sentence begins "I have eaten"; this is what's called the present perfect verb tense, and it is often used to describe an action that was completed in the past but remains true to the present moment. The action is part of history, not part of the continuous present, but, usually, when the action happened is not as important as the result of the action: e.g., I have taken that course or passed that exam. You might not know how to label verb tenses, but you do know how to use them in conversation and, probably, in writing. It may help to contrast "I have eaten" with choices the author could have made but didn't, such as "I eat." If they had said "I eat," the action would be characterized as ongoing (which might pose some problems as diction is usually impaired by talking while you are eating!). Also, the speaker might seem to be someone who reflects on all their actions and explores them for their significance. "I rise from bed, I approach the icebox, I open the door, I remove the plums, I eat them" is less about direct communication with another person and more about a person's acute, and perhaps excessive, preoccupation with themself. "I have eaten" is a report from one person to another.

The other sentence in the poem begins with "Forgive me," which is in what we call the imperative mood: it asks or commands the listener to do something. It can be used by a man talking to himself, for example, but even then it presumes there is some difference between the speaker and the listener, even if that listener is the same person as the speaker. (That sounds quite complicated, but, if you say "come on!" to yourself when you are biking up a steep hill, you are speaking as if there's part of yourself that can motivate the other part—you are speaking as if you are different from yourself! And that difference is the basis for communication.) Both of these aspects of the sentence structure underline that this is a communication between two people and that the intention of the communication is to describe action and transact emotion.

I'm beginning to think that "This Is Just To Say" is trying to tell us something about poetry, not just about plums. Perhaps it lacks those big-word features of poetry not by accident but as part of its desire to unsettle the difference we assume between ordinary, everyday communication and Poetry with a capital "P." Does "This Is Just To Say" want us to see instruction and delight in all kinds of communication, in every conversation, every piece of correspondence, every stray note and scrap of our daily life in words? Does it suggest that, if we keep our eyes and ears open, if we make ourselves ready to perceive, to feel, to speak, we can enjoy the world in the same way we can enjoy great poetry?

My notes on the technical features of "This Is Just To Say" may be more copious than yours; I've been trained, after all, to recognize these things, and I've read an awful lot of poetry in my time. But if you are careful to read every word of the work (especially when studying a short piece such as this poem), you will be able to see these features, even if you don't know the technical names for them. In your day-to-day life, you know the difference between a definite article and an indefinite article, and you make use of those differences in the way that you talk to others. You can ask your teacher or a classmate what these things are called if you notice them, or you can just describe them in your essay as best you can. But, believe me, if you or any other student were to analyze in an essay the effect of the definite articles in "This Is Just To Say" on the meaning or power or structure of the poem, I would be mighty impressed and interested. So take notes about how things are said and the kinds of words that are used, and think about how those choices shape the way that the literature you are studying works. Again, careful attention, close reading, and detailed notes will pay off when it comes time to write your essay.

TECHNIQUE

Technical features of literary works are fun to analyze. It's like watching amazing athletes and thinking about how they can do what they can do, all the tiny adjustments, capacities, and efforts that make their performances superior and even unique.

What Is the Work about?

Finally, we are ready for this question. You'll notice that I've put it after the others about our first impressions, even though it's often the thing we want to know first. This is because I really want you to try to be open to the text rather than going at it with a sense of what it's about. In my experience, as a literary critic myself and as a teacher, deciding what a work of literature means too early in my evidence-gathering process limits the evidence I gather to material that supports what I think the work is about. Also, what I think the work is about on first reading or—worse—because of its reputation or just from its title is bound to be narrower and less interesting than what the complex and multifaceted work is really about. If I read *Hamlet*, or see a production, just seeking clues to how and why the lead character delays or whether he loves his mother too much, I'm bound to miss much more than I notice.

That said, our very first impressions of the meaning of a work are important to keep track of, and you could write them down now. Grasping the surface or immediate meaning of a work of literature is essential to understanding how its complexity and depths work. My first reading of "This Is Just To Say" tells me that it is about some plums that the speaker ate and that they are asking another person, who seems to share an interest in or right to the plums, for forgiveness. You probably said something like that too. You are unlikely to forget this part of your reading, now that we've made a point of noticing it, but write it down anyway: your essay might well take shape in relation to it. For instance, many essays are structured around a difference between the surface meaning of a work of literature and the deeper meanings it contains. In this case, your essay might begin by saying, "On the surface, 'This Is Just To Say' is about some plums, an icebox, and two people, one of whom ate the plums the other one was saving"; then the essay might continue with an exploration of the deeper meanings and their relationship to this surface meaning. Deeper meanings are not necessarily more important or interesting than surface ones. In the case of "This Is Just To Say," for instance, you might want to write that the surface is the most important part of this poem, that our desire to see deeper meaning in everything is exactly what the poem thwarts:

the poem, like the plum, is "delicious," "sweet," and "cold," and it may want us to savor its taste and not worry about its digestion. But works of literature typically have more than one dimension of meaning, and essays often explore the relationship between them.

Before answering the question of what the deeper meanings of the poem are, I'd like you to look over your notes from the previous questions. Read over the key words you've listed, the feelings that the poem has given you, your notes about your identification with one or more of the people represented in the poem, and the list you've made of its technical features. We're going to go back to our evidence from our close reading when we construct our argument in Chapter Six, but, for now, let's see where we are.

Let's summarize here what I recorded during my close reading.

1. I like the poem.
2. The poem's vocabulary includes concrete nouns ("plums" and "icebox") and expressive adjectives ("delicious" and "sweet") that suggest it is about the real, material world.
3. It uses pronouns ("I" and "you"), indicating that it represents an act of communication between two people.
4. It gives me the following feelings:
   a. sensual pleasure
   b. awareness of potential for moral reflection
   c. awareness of overhearing an intimate communication
   d. admiration for the poet
5. I recognize four people represented in the poem with whom I identify:
   a. the speaker
   b. the person to whom the note is written
   c. the poet
   d. the implied reader
6. It includes the present perfect tense, the imperative mood, and definite articles. These affect the kind of communication the poem represents: it's a story about an action that's already complete, it asks or commands the spouse or roommate to do something, and it is oriented to the material world.

7. It follows the form of a note between two people rather than a poem. And, according to this form, it uses everyday language, even though it's a poem and poetry traditionally uses elevated language.

My notes include all the lines and words that support these observations. Reviewing them makes it clear to me that "This Is Just To Say" is not just about some plums, an icebox, and two people, one of whom ate the plums the other one was saving. There are three statements that I'm prepared to make now that I think might lead further as I make progress on my essay.

1. "This Is Just To Say" is about sensual, moral, and interpersonal experience in the material, everyday world.
2. "This Is Just To Say" is about relationships between people and about how these relationships are shaped by the use of language.
3. "This Is Just To Say" is about poetry and how it is different or the same as everyday acts of communication.

Those statements are based on my close reading of the poem and on a review of my notes about that reading. For most essays or for writing an essay-style answer on an exam about this poem, I've done half the work I have to do, so being patient and taking careful notes have been well worth it. I can now proceed to explore any further avenues of research I think are interesting, or I can go straight to organizing my evidence and ideas into an argument. My close reading has taught me a lot about how "This Is Just To Say" instructs, delights, and imitates life in its twelve short lines.

CONCLUSION

Your first impressions are very important. Your ideas will change in the course of your research, and you may even revise some of your initial ideas. But many of them will stay with you and gain in richness and complexity as you gather more knowledge about the work you are writing about. Taking the time to make your first impressions explicit and to express them in sentence form helps clarify them and can often help you consciously build on them as you continue your work toward your final essay.

Students often like to discuss their ideas for an essay with their teachers, and teachers sometimes require that they do so. In my experience, I can be most helpful to a student once their reading and thinking is at this point: the student can clearly state what their ideas are and can support those ideas with evidence from the text, if they are ones I haven't thought of before. At this stage, I can use my experience and knowledge to help make connections, suggest arguments, and offer leads for further research more easily than I can if the student has less specific thoughts to offer. If you like to consult with your instructor, or your instructor requires you to do so, now is a good time.

REVIEW QUESTIONS

1. Does it matter if you like the work of literature you are studying?
2. What are some of the ways in which a writer can generate feelings in their reader?
3. Why are technical features important to our study of literature?
4. Why is your first sense of the meaning of a work important, even if it's not quite "right"?
5. Is all literature about the writing of literature, in one way or another? Why is this interesting or important?

CHAPTER THREE

Using
Reference Works

AFTER OUR CLOSE READING EXPERIENCE, OUTLINED IN Chapter Two, we might have further questions that we'd like answers to before we proceed to writing our essay about "This Is Just To Say." I'm curious, for example, about whether any of the words we've noticed can be considered *symbols*—nouns or phrases that have abstract as well as concrete meanings that have developed over time. I'm also wondering how this poem compares with others by Williams—perhaps there are plums in other poems, perhaps he wrote more than one poem in the form of everyday communication, or perhaps he often represents intimate relationships. I'd sure like to know what an "icebox" is and when they were used. I'm motivated to learn more about Williams himself and about his career as a writer. I'd like to know if this poem was much noticed when it was first published, for example, and whether Williams was well known as a poet in general. For answers to these questions, I'll begin—and possibly end—with reference works.

Reference works are publications that include generally accepted facts and interpretations of historical and scientific information. They aren't always right, and they never contain the whole truth about a topic (we can't have everything right all the time, and we never know everything there is to know about something), but we trust these sources to give us answers that are plausible to experts and scholars around the world. Reference works are the first place to go if you are going to do research outside the text. The information they contain can be matched up easily with the evidence you have already collected and used to strengthen your essay when you write it.

How can you tell if a reference work is reliable? If it's in your library or available virtually through your library, then that library has endorsed it—not as containing the gospel truth but as a credible and reliable source for the kind of information it contains. Works that are recommended by your instructor should also be considered dependable. If these endorsements aren't available, then look for a reputable publishing house (you can search for it on the web, read about its history, and check out its other publications), and try to find editors and scholars with expertise in the area (you can search their names, either on the web or in specialized databases that we will explore in Chapter Five).

In this chapter, we'll look at how to get evidence for your essay from three kinds of sources: the *Oxford English Dictionary*, scholarly editions of the works of the author that you are studying, and encyclopedias. These three types of sources will be invaluable to you as you continue your studies.

THE *OXFORD ENGLISH DICTIONARY*

The *OED*, as it is called, is one of the most important basic resources for the study of English literature and the English language. It is normally available in university and college libraries in both printed and electronic forms. The print version is 20 volumes long and takes up a whole shelf in the library. The electronic version is easily accessible, and there is a tutorial within it to help you learn to use it. The library staff will also be happy to help you learn to use this rich resource. It's not hard, and it will help you write essays in English studies and in other humanities disciplines.

FORM AND FUNCTION

Make sure you get the right "part of speech" or grammatical term when you look up a word in the OED. *Many, many words in English can be both nouns and verbs or nouns and adjectives, for example, without any change in spelling: "plum," for instance, is both a noun and an adjective. ("Plumb" is a verb and an adverb, so someone who has plumbed the depths of the ocean can be plumb tuckered out.) Can you think of other words that have multiple functions?*

The OED offers three distinct perspectives on individual words that are helpful to us. First, it tells us the etymology or origin of the word. Second, it gives us definitions, with great precision. Third, it illustrates definitions with examples from written works, including literary, philosophical, historical, and legal works as well as newspapers and magazines. Using the online version of the OED makes gathering evidence extremely easy.

Etymology

English is a hybrid language, based on Saxon or Old English (a Germanic language) but with influxes from French, Greek, and Latin. When the Normans conquered England in 1066, they brought their dialect of French with them. Between the eleventh and the early fifteenth centuries, French was the language of the court, the government, and the law. In fact, each of those three words—"court," "government," and "law"—comes directly into English from French. To some degree, there is still a class division between Saxon-rooted words in English and French-rooted words: some people eat lunch at home, for instance, and others eat supper at a restaurant. Words of Saxon origin are often of one or two syllables, and they often signify the basic needs of life: "home," "love," "hearth," "food," "fight," "sword," "stone," "wood," and so on. Anglo-Norman words tend to be longer, and they often signify social customs and practices, status and reputation, and material goods beyond those that are essential to survival: "festival," "aristocrat," and "fork" are all examples.

SUGAR IN YOUR COFFEE?

Words imported into English from Arabic include "candy,"
"coffee," "giraffe," "guitar," "lime," "rice," "sugar," and "zero."
Some of these things were commodities that were traded;
others were part of the knowledge that got traded with sugar,
coffee, and rice. The words came with the traders, travelers,
scholars, and diplomats from many different countries who
spoke Arabic and other languages and used Arabic words when
communicating (about giraffes and candy, over a cup of coffee!)
with non-Arabic speakers. After the invention of the print-
ing press in the mid-fifteenth century, the absorption of these
imported words into other languages was accelerated.

Because education and information in the Renaissance were
international, English also absorbed many words from languages
such as Latin, Italian, Dutch, Spanish, and Arabic between 1500
and 1700. Greek-rooted words in English came with Greek texts that
were circulated in the Renaissance; as Greek knowledge of architecture, medicine, philosophy, and astronomy was considered the best,
our current vocabularies for those topics are words of Greek origin.
Law and politics were areas of Roman expertise, and the words that
we use in those areas come from Latin, whether they entered directly from Latin texts or from Latinate (or Romance) languages such
as French. So every word in English has a history. Literary writers
are often aware—sometimes unconsciously—of these origins and
make use of them when they choose their words. In "This Is Just
To Say," for example, the prevalence of short words of Saxon origin
("sweet," "cold," "plum," "I," and "you") reinforces our sense of the
poem as being about the material world and about basic relationships within that world between people and things and between
people and other people.

The origin of words may satisfy your curiosity more than it contributes to your essay directly, but it is always worth remembering
that English is a relatively young language (compared to Arabic,
Urdu, or Farsi) that is international in origin. The international flavor of English connects it to history in a very concrete way: giraffes

were icons of the exotic, signaling the great differences between landscape, climate, and culture between England and Africa, and the appearance of this word in late-sixteenth-century English shows that the exchange of knowledge and goods between faraway lands was well underway by that time. The history of the word "sugar" is a microscopic version of the trade in one of the world's most important commodities, a trade that led to the enrichment of nations, the enslavements of peoples, and the development of European colonies around the world. "Bungalow" and "khaki" are words that come into English as a result of British imperial rule over India during the nineteenth and twentieth centuries. The histories of words are great stories in and of themselves, and they may help you untangle the dense thickets of language that literary writers sometimes weave.

HWÆR BEOÞ WĒ

(WITH SOMETHING THAT LOOKS LIKE A SHOVEL?)

I also notice, as I'm sure you will, that Old English (OE) is a different language altogether, with different letterforms! It's something you would have to be taught to read. It's a good adventure, learning Old English, but not something you are expected to be able to do to make use of the OED. It is interesting and meaningful when authors choose words with OE roots, and you don't need to be able to pronounce the OE words to make use of this fact. (By the way, "hwær beoþ wē" can be translated into more modern English as "where we are.")

Definitions

The definitions of words can change and multiply over time. The *OED* records all the known definitions of English words. The electronic version is updated frequently, so new definitions of old words and new coinages are added often. You'll be surprised by how many definitions most words have: try looking up "pen," "desk," "paper," or "book" to see that the common props of student life have rich and varied meanings. I can't stress too much what a great treasure trove your language is, and the *OED* puts it all on display.

"Plum," one of the key words we've identified in "This Is Just To Say," is a pretty straightforward word. If we look first under "plum, *n.* and *adj.*" in the *OED*, we'll find that the word is Germanic and that the first meaning is just what we think it is from the poem: an edible fruit "usually having purple, red, or yellow skin with a dull powdery bloom when ripe, a sweet pulp, and a flattish pointed stone." The word can also refer to the plum tree or to the wood of the plum tree. There are a couple of other definitions that might or might not be of interest. For instance, perhaps Williams wanted a word that could also mean "a coveted prize; the pick of a collection of things" ("plum, *n.*" 5c)—the plums in "This Is Just To Say" are clearly the most desirable things in the icebox. I don't think he meant "testicles," which is another definition, as saving them for breakfast doesn't really make culinary or cultural sense. If there were other words in the poem that implied body parts or genitals (or if "rocks," "nuts," "balls," "stones," or "family jewels" also appeared in the poem!) I might think again about this definition, but I don't see anything like that, so I will discard that definition as a possible one.

TURDUCKEN? NO THANKS

The day I wrote this section, the front page of the electronic OED *featured four words newly added to the dictionary: "bailout," "car-booter," "rechallenge," and "turducken." These words aren't necessarily brand new: in fact, for "bailout," the entry shows that the word was used as early as 1939, with the same meaning it has today. By the way, a "turducken, n." is a "poultry dish consisting of a boned chicken inside a boned duck which is in turn placed inside a (partially) boned turkey, along with seasoned stuffing between the layers of meat and in the central cavity, the whole typically being cooked by roasting." Perhaps that makes your mouth water and your stomach rumble; I won't join you on that one, either at dinner or supper!*

One of the definitions of "plum" that intrigues me helps to explain to me why the plums I imagine the poem to be describing are purple, rather than red or yellow, both perfectly acceptable colors for plums. Definition #7 for "plum" is a "reddish-purple colour characteristic of some plums." This does give me some insight into the poem. Banana, apple, pineapple, gooseberry—those are not colors. "Plum" means both the fruit and the color of some of the fruit; my imaginary plum is purple because the color plum is purple. Williams has chosen a fruit that is more readily visualized than others, one that therefore appears concrete and real to the reader. As concrete and real are both qualities of the scene that Williams sets in the poem, and because the visual is one of the senses and this is a sensual poem, "plum" is a great choice for "This Is Just To Say."

If I look up "plum" as an adjective, which I'm encouraged to do by the fact that the plums must be "plum" colored, I will find more information that backs up my sense that Williams has chosen an especially sensual type of fruit. "Plum" also means "plump" ("plum, *adj*.1" 1), and the examples (I get ahead of myself!) suggest that this definition usually applied to desirable female flesh. This definition emphasizes the sensual and intimate atmosphere of the poem. The next definition of the adjective is "soft, yielding" ("plum, *adj*.1" 2a); the examples suggest that it was usually applied in this sense to rocks and cakes, but I can still argue that the word "plum," because the flesh of the fruit is plump, soft, and yielding, carries the association of physical desire and pleasure as well. The adjectival form of "plum" therefore enhances the sensual dimension of the poem and suggests that the relationship between the people represented in the poem has an erotic quality. As I had a vague sense that the poem had an erotic dimension, I'm glad to see that my work in the dictionary is reinforcing that perception.

MORE ON PLUMS

If you look up "plum" as an adjective in the OED you'll see that the first definition (plump) is identified as "obsolete" and the second (soft) is labeled "regional." It's important to recognize that these meanings were not the most common or likely for English-speaking people at the time the poem was written. But poets know language like painters know paint and electricians know electricity, and we should expect poets to draw on the history of language—even as they contribute to its future.

You can look up other key words that we identified to see if their definitions enrich your understanding of why the poet chose them and how they work to help create a powerful experience for the reader. "Sweet" and "cold" both have sensual and emotional dimensions, for instance. "Breakfast" comes from "breaking" and "fast," or eating after a time of not eating, and the word can have a ritual or ceremonial meaning. This may suggest that the speaker is aware of having disturbed the customary practices of his world and within his relationship with the person who is hearing or reading the "note" about the plums. The request for forgiveness is not just for having eaten the plums, we can conclude, but also for breaking the customary habits and forms of communion within the world of the poem. The speaker is not as serious as I am making him out to be—in asking for forgiveness, a legal and even theological term, for something so petty as eating the plums, he's exaggerating the transgression. But, at the same time, he may be elevating the everyday habits of his relationship, giving them a spiritual or transcendent gloss. This enhancement of the familiar would be in synch with how he raises an everyday form of communication to the status of poetry, so I'm thinking that I might be onto something here. I'll put it in my evidence file, along with the other observations that I've noticed.

A NOTE ON NOTES

When you take notes from the Oxford English Dictionary, *make sure you write down the heading for the entry you are quoting from or paraphrasing (for example, "plum, adj.1") and the number of the definition within the entry (for example, 2a).*

Examples of Usage

The OED offers a third type of information: examples for each definition of the use of the word through the ages. This feature is especially helpful when you are working on literature from the more distant past: for instance, if you are writing an essay about *Hamlet,* you will find definitions and examples that were current in Shakespeare's time, which can really help you understand exactly how the play works and what passages mean. These usage examples may also help you to identify symbols (that is, words that have abstract meanings beyond the concrete things they refer to) and allusions (references to the works of other literary writers). The examples of usage in the *OED* can be a quick shortcut to a deep insight about the literary work you are studying.

"Sweet" is an old and rich word with many meanings that are relevant to our analysis of "This Is Just To Say." "Sweet" can refer to flavor, to scent, or to sound; to foods or flowers; and to emotions and actions. Again, with this choice, Williams is emphasizing the sensual and erotic dimensions of the relationship depicted in the poem, within which the plums have taken on such power and beauty. But there is more information that might be relevant here in the examples of usage. Let's look more closely at them and at what they can tell us about "This Is Just To Say."

Under "sweet, *a.* and *adv.*" in the *OED*, the first meaning is as follows:

> *1. a.* Pleasing to the sense of taste; having a pleasant taste or flavour ... having the characteristic flavour (ordinarily pleasant when not in excess) of sugar, honey, and many ripe fruits, which corresponds to one of the primary sensations of taste. Also said of the taste or flavour. Often opposed to *bitter* or *sour*....

Nothing much surprises me about this definition, which is what I thought "sweet" meant in the context of the poem. But when I skim through the examples of the usage, I notice one that really interests me.

It's a quotation from John Milton's epic poem *Paradise Lost*. (The reference is abbreviated in some versions of the *OED* as "Milton *P.L.*" However, if I click on the name "Milton," I get to a list of his titles, *Paradise Lost* among them.) The quotation is this: "O Fruit Divine, Sweet of thy self, but much more sweet thus cropt," and it comes from Book V of the poem (which has 12 books), beginning with line 68. There's an online version of *Paradise Lost* maintained at a site called *The Milton Reading Room*, and I look up the quotation there. That way I can insert the line breaks, which are missing from the OED quotation, and I can also use the search function on my browser to look for the word "sweet" in the rest of Book V of the poem. Because I teach *Paradise Lost* and do research on Milton's works, I'm quite familiar with the poem, and I know something about the context for the quotation: Eve is recounting to Adam the dream that she has had that Satan put in her head. In the dream, an angelic form eats the fruit from the tree that has been forbidden to Adam and Eve (the Tree of Knowledge of Good and Evil) and claims that it has given him the knowledge of the gods. In the dream, Eve also intends to eat the fruit, but she wakes before she does.

Because I know about the context and have studied the poem so closely, I have a bit of an unfair advantage here. I know the fruit is forbidden, that the angelic form is Satan in disguise, that the fruit is eaten, that this transgression constitutes original sin, and that the whole drama is played out with the focus on the relationship between Adam and Eve. But even if you don't know this, you may well be familiar with the story of the forbidden fruit and original sin. Or you may ask your instructor if they think there is any relationship between the fruit in the passage from *Paradise Lost* and the fruit in "This Is Just To Say"; they are likely to answer that it is certainly possible that Williams wants us to remember the association between forbidden fruit, transgression, and punishment. You can decide if that association is ironic, in that he's foisting a mythological and moralistic story onto a simple and everyday situation, thus implying a connection between the most solemn of discourses and the note on the kitchen table, but that's all to the good: your analysis will be richer for such thinking.

You might decide, on reflection and after this research, that the plums in "This Is Just To Say" are a *symbol*. Symbols in literature are words that represent things but also have meaning beyond the things themselves. For instance, worms connote death, flowing water can mean time, and germinating seeds often signal life and growth. Symbols start because the thing is associated with an abstract or complex phenomenon, but they gain their power and importance through repeated use within literature. In literature, we can usually tell if a worm means death or is just a worm by the context.

One of the interesting things to note about "This Is Just To Say" is that it doesn't feature flowing water or growing plants: it doesn't rely on images to convey its meanings in the way that some other poems do. A lot of poems play with traditional images and undermine their conventional meanings. Think of Shakespeare's sonnet that begins "My mistress' eyes are nothing like the sun" ("Sonnet 130"), for example; it challenges the way in which poets lazily use tired images of natural splendor to describe their lovers' beauty. But the connection that the dictionary has revealed to us between the poem by Williams and the Judeo-Christian myth of original sin may signal that the plums in "This Is Just To Say" are symbols of something beyond the material fruit, purple and sweet and cold as they are. As I've said, Williams may be using the image ironically—he may even be making fun of how poets use images to refer to concepts and expect their readers to know what they're talking about. But still the line of thought is interesting. Perhaps we juxtapose everyday thinking and action against moralistic thinking and mythological action when we are aware of the potential for the plums to be a symbol—and perhaps that set of thoughts is one of the things we take away from reading the poem.

Your notes from the dictionary can be filed separately from your notes from the close reading such as we undertook in Chapter Two. But tag them with terms that will allow you to line them up with the parts of the poem to which they pertain. Imagine you are building a database, even a spreadsheet, which will integrate evidence from the work you are studying with evidence from reference sources such as the *Oxford English Dictionary*. Remember that your plan is to assemble enough evidence that writing your essay will simply be a matter of explaining and accounting for the evidence in relation to your overall argument. So document carefully and thoroughly, and label your files and tag your notes clearly.

SCHOLARLY EDITIONS

One of the most important contributions that scholars make to our understanding of literature and the worlds in which it is created and consumed is the preparation of scholarly editions. To use an example, Shakespeare's plays were published without his oversight and often from copies that had been used on the stage or that were made on the basis of actors' reports to printers. There are great lines in Shakespeare's plays that we will never know the origin of, for sure. An example is Juliet's "rose" speech in *Romeo and Juliet*: the version we are confident that Shakespeare had a direct hand in delivering to the printer reads "a rose by any other *word* would smell as sweet," while the version that we love and admire as Shakespeare's was probably recited (imperfectly) by an actor who had performed the play and reads "a rose by any other *name* would smell as sweet." Since the speech, as you know, is about names and the burdens they impose and not, more generally, about words and the ways in which they function, we like the second better. But a scholarly editor has to decide on which to put in the text that you read, and that decision has to be backed up by logic and research. This work can take years of patient investigating. Some of your instructors have devoted careers to scholarly editing.

In addition to printing more of the author's works than you might already have read, scholarly editions have three features that are of importance to you as a student of literature. The first is what I've already described: the scholarly editor makes decisions about what version of the work to print. Poems can be printed in magazines and early collections and then revised for inclusion in anthologies and collected works. Plays can change between page and stage. Novels can be serialized in magazines or revised for republication. Significant changes can occur in revisions, and those changes can affect how we interpret the works. Scholarly editors research these changes, figuring out which to include in their editions and then how to signal to readers that the changes occurred at some point in history.

WHY THAT BOOK IN PARTICULAR?

It may frustrate you that your instructor wants you to have a certain edition of a work for class. That edition may be more expensive or harder to get than other editions. But the instructor has good reasons: they want you to have a version of the text that has been prepared by a scholar, that has annotations, and that has an introduction. These are all valuable resources for the study of the literature you are reading in the course you are taking.

The second feature of scholarly editions is that they normally have annotations—footnotes or endnotes and sometimes marginal notes as well—that give the reader additional information about the text. In works that were written long ago, such as Shakespeare's plays, these notes often include definitions of archaic words. They may also identify allusions to other works or to mythological stories. In collections of poetry, they may give additional information about the first publications of the poem or the biographical or cultural context for the poem.

The third feature of a scholarly edition is the "Introduction." In order to prepare the edition, the scholar has had to read all of the author's works and many more from the same period; find out everything they can about the author's biography; survey the critical reception of the works since their first publication or circulation; and come to conclusions about how to interpret the work. The scholarly editor is the pre-eminent expert on the works of the author they have edited, and this knowledge is distilled in the introduction to the work you are studying. The introduction is the best place to start if you want to enlarge your understanding of the work and learn more about its genesis, its place in literary history, and the possibilities for interpretation that have been pursued by scholars over the years.

Scholarly editions are usually printed, but they are becoming increasingly available through library databases. If you are studying a work in an individual text recommended or required by your instructor, then you will usually have a scholarly edition; more are available in the library and will perhaps be listed in the edition that you have, as additional resources or references. If you are studying a work printed in an anthology, there should be information about the source of the work that the editors of the anthology used in the anthology.

The Collected Poems of William Carlos Williams, 1909–1939 has a lot of information that is valuable for our study of "This Is Just To Say." Even before the title page, there's a list of works by Williams, and I'm astonished and impressed at the number of individual volumes of poetry he published. He was a prolific and accomplished writer. There's a photo of him opposite the title page that shows me he was a white guy who could wear a suit and tie and easily bear an intelligent and thoughtful expression. The "Contents" list is ten pages long; there must be hundreds of poems in this book. The book is organized according to the volumes of poetry he published, although "This Is Just To Say" is in the section of poems that were published individually and did not appear in a collection. There is a "Preface" that describes the editorial process for the book and gives a little information about how Williams participated in the collection of his poems, but there is no "Introduction" that describes the life and literary career of the author; I'm quite disappointed about that, and I will have to find out more elsewhere. But there are annotations, and the note to "This Is Just To Say" is a gold mine of just the sort of information that is available only in a scholarly edition.

BEWARE!

To be completely honest with you, when I first thought of using "This Is Just To Say" for this section of Writing Essays About Literature, *I looked up the poem on the Internet and was sent to the digitized book library put online by a major search-engine company, where I found the poem. What really astonished me was that, when I went to look it up again a few days later, the digitized version of the 1986 edition of* The Collected Poems of William Carlos Williams, 1909–1939 *had disappeared. The second edition of the work, published in 1991, was only partly represented online, as only a few pages had been scanned. The lesson I've learned the hard way is this: at this point in time, non-scholarly digital libraries can sometimes be unreliable, and print resources and databases found through your university library are preferable.*

The note to "This Is Just To Say" tells me that Williams wrote a poem called "Reply" that was not published until 1982. In the *Collected Poems*, the editors print the version from Williams's typescript. It begins like this: "Dear Bill: I've made a / couple of sandwiches for you. / In the ice-box you'll find / blue-berries ..." (536). The subtitle of the poem is "crumpled on her desk," and the poem implies that this is the response by the speaker's wife to "This Is Just To Say." The poetic "Reply" ends "Love. Floss." and then "Please switch off the telephone." As a companion piece to "This Is Just To Say," "Reply" is rich—and quite hilarious. The sensuousness of "This Is Just To Say" is completely absent from "Reply": there are few adjectives, no "sweet" or "delicious," and "cold" is used to refer to "a glass of cold coffee"—one of the items in the icebox. There is also no moral dimension (no "forgive"). There are lots of definite articles—the world depicted is completely, almost relentlessly, material. The intersubjective relationship that is depicted is more prosaic than in the first poem: the speaker patiently explains how to make tea, as if the reader or listener is quite naïve or even somewhat underdeveloped intellectually. Read together with "This Is Just To Say," the second poem highlights the complexities and richness of the first poem. We might even say it comments ironically on the relationship between real-world communication (the note on the kitchen table) and poetry, a relationship that the first poem presents us with: whatever "This Is Just To Say" seems to think about the potential for poetry in everyday communications, "Reply" makes sure we remember that everyday writing is often lacking in feeling, sensuality, and intellectual interest.

Scholarly editions are treasure troves for students of literature. In addition to the fact that they may offer additional works by the same author (usually the case with scholarly editions of poetry), they compact years of research into manageable forms. They are always produced by people with exceptional expertise, and they are valued by libraries and scholars in the field. Whenever you have the chance, examine what we call the *apparatus* of the text: look at the table of contents, the statement of editorial principles, and the annotations, and read the "Introduction." Even if you don't use any of the information you gather directly in your essay, this reading will help you to better understand how literature happens historically, what literary scholars do, and how they present literature and literary scholarship to the reading public. As usual, take careful notes and label them with categories that relate to what you've already gathered as evidence from the poem. Also note any ideas you've had as you've been collecting evidence.

ENCYCLOPEDIAS

An encyclopedia is a work that collects knowledge at a general level on an exhaustive list of topics. Encyclopedias can be devoted to a single area of knowledge, so you will find encyclopedias about Japan, geology, or Judaism in your library, if it's anything like mine. There are specialist encyclopedias that relate to literary studies too, and you might find these useful for your research. In my library, *The Oxford Encyclopedia of American Literature*, the *Literary Encyclopedia*, and *The Oxford Companion to Twentieth-Century Poetry in English* are all listed under "Encyclopedias" in the online reference section of the library's website. Each of these will have something to offer about Williams and the literary history to which he belongs.

Such encyclopedias are very useful to the study of literature. The first thing that you might look up in an encyclopedia is the author's biography, which will contain information about their life and their career as a writer. Encyclopedias often also contain overviews of time periods, literary movements (such as transcendentalism or symbolism), literary forms (such as the elegy or the novel), and literary devices (such as alliteration or allusion) and terms (such as irony or melodrama).

Encyclopedias have been easily adapted to digital publication. These searchable and easily cross-referenced digital texts are even more useful and rich than print encyclopedias. Besides, the ease of updating digital texts means that the knowledge in digital encyclopedias is usually current; the wide availability and easy access to digital resources make online encyclopedias popular, and that popularity can drive quality higher. In fact, as I'm sure you know, the most popular encyclopedia used today is the digitally born *Wikipedia*. I believe I can say that if you are literate and have access to a computer, you have used *Wikipedia*. I doubt I could say that about any other site, except popular search engines.

Wikipedia has been the subject of some controversy in recent years, and there has been reluctance within academic institutions to accept its use as a source for student essays. Because *Wikipedia* has responded positively to criticisms—by making it harder for individuals to change articles without editorial intervention, for example, and by labeling questionable articles clearly—the quality has improved, and most instructors now allow students to use it (and use it often themselves for quick facts and explanations!). I allow students to use it, and, in fact, I prefer them to use *Wikipedia* rather than other question-answering services on the web, which do not have as stringent quality controls as *Wikipedia* does (and often just copy what *Wikipedia* contains, sometimes inaccurately and often partially). You can read more about *Wikipedia* in various places; the article in the *Wikipedia* about the *Wikipedia* is actually very helpful, quite balanced, and contains a number of links and references to other accounts. You should check with your instructor as to whether you are allowed to use *Wikipedia* in your essays. Other general and specialized encyclopedias are available through your library's portal, and you can turn to them for information. Here I'm going to refer to the *Wikipedia* article about William Carlos Williams as my example.

You'll remember that the scholarly edition of Williams's poems, our source for "This Is Just To Say," does not have much in the way of a biography of the poet. The *Wikipedia* article, on the other hand, has lots of biographical and literary historical information about him. He was born in New Jersey, and he was a doctor. He was acquainted with other great poets of his era, such as Ezra Pound, Hilda Doolittle (known as H.D.), Marianne Moore, Wallace Stevens, Charles Olson, Robert Creeley, and Allen Ginsberg, and with artists such as Man Ray and Marcel Duchamp. There's a lot of information in the article about his ideas of poetry and technique, and a little information about his politics and personal life. The article doesn't say if he was well regarded during his lifetime, although it looks as if other poets took him very seriously, but it does say that he was awarded the Pulitzer Prize and other major honors after his death.

When you take notes from an Internet source, you should make sure to write down the date on which you took the note. The reason for this is that Internet sources, unlike books and journals, can be altered between the time that you use them and the time that your quotation is read by your instructor or peer. Also make sure to copy the URL exactly, even if the citation style you are using doesn't require it. Last, I'd like to emphasize that while Internet resources are terrific, your instructors will prefer ones that are available through the library and others that they approve. General resources on the web contain many errors, are unstable, and are often subjective in a way that is interesting for us as readers but not useful to us as scholars and critics. If you would like to look at other reference works that are relevant to English studies, look at the list of electronic handbooks, encyclopedias, and dictionaries that your librarian has identified as relevant to English studies. Most college and university libraries produce extensive research guides for every academic discipline taught at the school, and these describe the reference works for that subject and how to use them. Or talk to a librarian yourself. Librarians know an awful lot that can help you in your work.

CYBER-VANDALISM?

If you click on the "history" tab of a Wikipedia *page, you can see the history of additions and revisions to the article that you are reading. The* Wikipedia *community is quite rigorous in its efforts to catch and reverse malicious or erroneous additions to articles, and you can see those actions recorded in the log. Click on "talk" next to any username, and you will find out more. In fact, in preparing the second edition of this book, I found that the entry on Williams had been significantly revised! That's why we should always include the date we accessed digital resources.*

CONCLUSION

My research in these reference works has led me to several insights that I will write down in my list of great ideas that I have had.

1. From the dictionary, I learned (or was reminded) that a plum is a fruit and a color. Perhaps I can say that Williams's choice of words emphasizes the many sensual dimensions of the fruit: the color, the appearance, the feel ("cold"), and the taste. (The only sense missing is hearing. I guess you can't hear plums.)

2. From the dictionary, I learned that most of the words that are used in the poem derive from Old English and are older and simpler words compared to others in modern English.

3. From the scholarly edition, I confirmed that the poem is in a style written as if it were a note to his wife (he wrote a "Reply" to it in her voice) and that it was written in 1934.

4. From the biographical article, I learned that Williams was a doctor, a father, and that he and Florence (Floss) were married for decades.

I'll add these notes to the ones I collected after my close reading. I have a sense that my insights are growing and that I'm going to be able to write a good essay.

You might be ready to write your essay now. Certainly, if I didn't want to go further, or didn't have to, I could stop here and write up a nice essay; it would have something to do with how the use of words in the poem reinforces the themes I perceive (of sensual experience, of communication between two people, and of intimate life). You might want to see my attempt at doing this in Sample Essay One (pp. 169–76). If you are not supposed to go beyond reference works in your research, you can skip to Chapter Six, in which we will discuss how to put together the essay from the evidence you have collected. If you want to do research in social and historical contexts, however, you should go on to the next chapter.

REVIEW QUESTIONS

1. How do you know if a reference work is a suitable source for an essay?

2. What are the three main things that we can learn about words from the *OED*?

3. What are the features of a scholarly edition?

4. What is the potential value of reading other works by the author you are writing your essay about?

5. What do you and your classmates think about using *Wikipedia*? What does your instructor think?

6. How do you think the biography of authors might be useful in the study of literature?

CHAPTER FOUR

Research about Social and Historical Contexts

LITERATURE IS PRODUCED IN SOCIETIES AND WITHIN history. In many ways, literature is a group effort: it uses language, which is the common property of everyone in the society, and it requires not just writers but readers. Literature reflects the values, beliefs, and perceptions of the world in which it was produced, and it can also contribute to shaping or altering those. Readers, as much as writers, make literature what it is: they interpret it, share it, talk about it, critique it, and imitate it. The language from literature enters into other discourses: think, for example, of terms such as "Big Brother" or phrases such as "To be or not to be," which have become commonplaces in our communication, even for people who have never actually read *Nineteen Eighty-Four* or seen a performance of *Hamlet*.

Literary critics often work to place literature in social contexts. But social contexts are very broad. How do you know what aspects to pursue? How do you find good-quality, relevant information? And how do you incorporate the information you find into your analysis of the literature you are studying? This chapter will explore these questions.

In this chapter, we'll again use the example of William Carlos Williams's poem "This Is Just To Say." You can reread it now; you'll find it at the beginning of Chapter Two (p. 19).

TOPICS FOR RESEARCH: SOCIAL PHENOMENA AND LITERARY MOVEMENTS

Understanding literature in its social and historical context is an infinitely productive mode of interpretation, and one that most academic literary critics practice in some form or another. But academic literary critics may take years (and get paid!) to troll through archives, read thousands of documents, and arrange and rearrange their evidence in order to produce critical works that situate literature in its time period and social context in a way that illuminates the literature. How can you interpret literature in terms of its historical and social contexts, given that you have lots of other courses, limited time in which to work on the project, and many interests and obligations?

The key is to stick close to the works you are studying and the author or authors of those works. Allowing yourself to be guided by the work (and other works by the author, if they are a manageable length for you to read) will help narrow the field of choices you have and ensure that your research is relevant to the works you are studying. Even so, works will give you a wide range of areas to investigate. Literary works are always about topics we know have a social history: marriage, for example, or exploration, or space travel, or class relations, or theories of the mind. *Hamlet*, *Pride and Prejudice*, and Pat Barker's *Regeneration* trilogy are all set in wartime, and research about that topic will help you to understand how characters behave, their priorities and pressures, and how conflicts are resolved and pleasures are portrayed. *King Lear* and *The Stone Angel* are about aging, and aging itself has a history: in different times and different social situations we perceive the elderly differently, and they in turn perceive themselves in relation to social attitudes toward that group. *Uncle Tom's Cabin*, *The Color Purple*, and *Things Fall Apart* are all about race as both a way of organizing a society and a personal characteristic that affects how people perceive themselves and act within a society.

Beyond the works themselves, the author's biography will give you clues as to profitable areas of investigation. Author biographies are found in encyclopedias and reference works, in biographies published as books, and, often, in introductions to scholarly editions of an author's works. From information about the authors in biographies, you can select topics to research further. Nadine Gordimer, winner of the Booker Prize in 1974 for her novel *The Conservationist*, was a member of the African National Congress for decades; there's lots of information about the ANC, about apartheid, and about resistance to apartheid in South Africa that's readily available to you in reference works. Henry James, whose novels *Daisy Miller* and *The Portrait of a Lady* are intensely focused on the consciousness of their sensitively drawn female protagonists, had a brother William James, who was a psychologist. Is it any wonder that Henry's understanding of character was influenced by contemporary theories of the mind? Kurt Vonnegut, author of *Slaughterhouse-Five* (and many other works that blend satire and science fiction), was a soldier and a prisoner of war in World War II, and his experiences contributed to his representation of war and the suffering of those who were involved with it. Using biographies and reference works, you can pinpoint a few of the issues associated with an author's historical context that interest you and that you feel have a presence in their work.

Authors are also often involved in literary movements and communities. Literary movements are founded on aesthetic principles, and members of those communities will often articulate the values they share and try to promote in their works. These can be content-based values—for instance, Romantic poets were committed to representing the lives of real working people. Or they can be technical and aesthetic values: Romantic poets were also committed to using the language that people spoke rather than the elevated and removed "poetic" language conventional to the works of their predecessors. Most authors belong, either actively and consciously or passively and without explicit engagement, to aesthetic movements and groupings. T.S. Eliot was associated with

Ezra Pound, Wyndham Lewis, and James Joyce, each of whom influenced Eliot's work. bpNichol, the Canadian poet, was connected with Robert Creeley, Charles Olson, and the Black Mountain poets, and comparing his work with the values they articulate in their statements about "projective verse" (a form of poetry that was to be based on how people speak and breathe, not on traditional concepts of meter and rhythm) would be a productive exercise. Zora Neale Hurston was part of what is now called the Harlem Renaissance (it was called the New Negro Movement at the time), which sought to represent the lives and circumstances of African Americans in forms and language that were closer to their experience and less determined by the attitudes and presumptions of white people and their literature. Again, you can use biographies to identify aesthetic movements and artistic communities with which the author you are studying was associated, and then you can investigate these further in reference works and books from the library.

THE INTENTIONAL FALLACY

In 1946, W.K. Wimsatt and Monroe Beardsley published the first version of their essay called "The Intentional Fallacy." In this essay, they argue that "the design or intention of the author is neither available nor desirable as a standard for judging the success of a work of literary art" (3) and that speculation about the author belongs to literary biography—not literary criticism. Like other New Critics, Wimsatt and Beardsley believe that critics should examine the work itself exclusively. Close reading is always valuable and often sufficient. But critics nowadays like to look to context to see if it helps to explain the choices the writer has made and the effect the work of literature has on its readers. Still, Wimsatt and Beardsley are right in one way: never assume that the voice of a literary work is identical with that of its author. Authors are craftspeople; poems and novels are things they make—they are not simply shout-outs.

USEFUL RESOURCES

However small your library, it will offer you a range of useful resources for research in social and historical contexts relevant to English studies. Some of these resources are in print, but many are in digital form. Many of the digital resources that your library offers are not available for all users of the Internet: they are subscriptions, and the library pays for you to have access to them. So take some time to familiarize yourself with the digital resources provided by your library.

Digital resources have changed the practice of research for all levels of students of literature. Facsimiles (exact copies, usually photographic) and transcriptions (copies that duplicate the words but not the material features of the texts in question) of works that used to be available only to the most privileged and dedicated scholars can now be used by anyone with access to particular databases. Works that existed in single copies (letters, manuscripts, rare printed documents) and that may have been seen or read previously by only a handful of people are now widely distributed in facsimile. Bodies of work and collections of texts can be searched, organized, and compared in ways that were not possible before the age of the computer.

DATABASES AT MY LIBRARY

My library at the University of Waterloo subscribes to a number of digital resources that can help with the study of the social and historical contexts of literature. They include Eighteenth Century Journals, *a digital facsimile of serial publications issued between 1685 and 1815;* North American Women's Letters and Diaries, *which includes transcriptions of letters and diaries by women of North America, searchable by many different criteria, including date range and location; and* Defining Gender, *a collection of digital facsimiles, supplemented by topical essays, which illuminate all aspects of the social construction and experience of gender in the English-speaking world between 1450 and 1910. Check out resources such as these through your library's interface.*

Most of these resources have definitions that limit them to places, languages, time periods, and topics. The titles of the resources give a brief indication of their contents. But the richness of these databases must be explored to be believed. *Early English Books Online* has more than 100,000 photographic facsimiles of books and pamphlets printed before 1700. *North American Immigrant Letters, Diaries, and Oral Histories* includes 2,162 authors, approximately 100,000 pages of information, and a collection of audio files that pertain to the experience of immigration to America between 1800 and 1950. Each of these databases offers a unique perspective on its subject area, and having a look through both will help you with your work and open your eyes to the tremendous riches that are available to scholars and students of all types.

USING YOUR FINDINGS

As we found out from his biography, William Carlos Williams was associated with a large number of other poets, novelists, and visual artists during his long career and with several literary movements, including modernism, beat poetry, and the Black Mountain school. Most famously, he was part of the movement called "imagism," which—like so many poetic movements before it—sought to use language that was common to social discourse and aimed to represent reality and the experience of it in ways that were more direct and sensual and less moralistic and ideological than had been the case in the poetry of the previous generation. There are articles on imagism in reference works. You can consult, for example, *The Oxford Companion to Twentieth-Century Poetry in English*, which is available online; an article on *Wikipedia* that is quite helpful; and various mentions in several articles in the online *Johns Hopkins Guide to Literary Theory and Criticism*. Williams's famous dictum was "no ideas but in things," which is from the opening section of his long poem *Paterson* (6). He elaborated on this idea in some of his essays, which are widely available in collected versions in libraries. One way to approach "This Is Just To Say" is to read it in terms of the aesthetic and social values that Williams tried to assert through his poetry. You might want to consider, in addition, a couple of his other poems, notably "The Red Wheelbarrow," which also expresses these values. If you were to go further afield, you might want to read some poetry and poetics (that is, prose that articulates a theory of poetry) by other authors with whom he was contemporary or associated; they will be listed in biographies and articles in reference works about Williams and about the literary movements to which he belonged.

There are other interesting leads in Williams's biography that might be worth following up. He lived through both world wars. He was born and lived for much of his life in New Jersey. He went to medical school and practiced as a family doctor for many years. He and his wife Florence (Flossie) had two sons. There are photographs in biographies and on the Internet that can give you a flavor of the period, a sense of Williams himself, and an impression about his context and surroundings.

As you search for the topic you will pursue, it's important to read more than you can possibly use. You must explore what is there in order to find that combination of what interests you and what connects with the literature that is at the center of your studies. When I write an essay, I usually look at about ten times as many books and articles as I actually quote in the essay, and I usually read about four times as many. That sounds inefficient, doesn't it? But really, I'm learning a lot as I go. There are three kinds of learning going on: one, I'm learning more about the time period or literary context in general; two, I'm learning what I don't want to write about, which is helpful in determining what I do want to write about; three, I'm learning what other people have said about what does interest me, and I may decide there is something missing from what they've said or that I want to say something different. You aren't expected to do as much skimming and reading as I do; this is my job, after all. But you should expect to look at three times as many works as you ultimately use and to read at least twice as much. The learning is good, in a general sense: that's what you're in school for. But you also hold on to your notes, and they may well come in handy for another assignment in another course.

There are many contexts for the poem that do interest me, but in order to make a decision, I have to go back to the poem, and to my notes on the poem, and go from there. When I return to "This Is Just To Say," I'm not struck by anything that will connect with war or medicine or New Jersey. What I am struck by—again—is the domestic nature of the setting (the "icebox," the note-like quality of the poem) and the intimacy of the communication. So I decide I'd like to investigate domestic and family life in the era of the poem. In my library's search interface, I type in "family AND America" as subjects, to get me started.

BOOLEAN OPERATORS

The "AND" in the middle of "family AND America" is called a Boolean operator, and it establishes that I want to retrieve only entries that have both *those terms in their subject descriptions. Inserting "or" instead would produce a list of items that have one or the other term in their subject descriptions. In advanced searches, you can construct longer Boolean strings, so that you can ask for "family AND America NOT 'upper class'"; this search would filter out all the items also tagged with the phrase "upper class." These tags are called "metadata"—meaning the data that is above the data of the text. The structure of metadata is one of the areas of scholarship and professional practice that will grow exponentially in the next few years; it's a good idea to figure out what it is!*

Diagram 1: Boolean Operators at Work

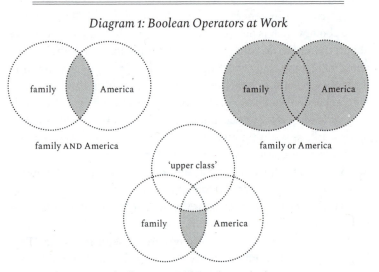

family AND America

family or America

family AND America NOT 'upper class'

I start with a book that has a title that fits my search criteria (in this case, *Family Life in 20th-Century America*), and then I look at the subject categories listed in its catalogue entry. From there, I go to the list of all the books that share that combination of subject categories ("Families – United States – History – 20th century"). There, I find another book that I request from my library system, *The "American Way": Family and Community in the Shaping of American Identity* by Allan Carlson. I also see a book called *Images of Family Life in Magazine Advertising, 1920–1978*. When I call up its catalogue entry, I look at the subject categories that it is tagged with and click on one of them that interests me ("Sex role in advertising – United States – History – 20th century"). I choose this subject heading because I'm interested not just in what people did but in how their lives were reflected back to them, idealized, or even criticized in media, and advertising is a great place to start. Looking under that subject category, I find another book that seems relevant to me; it's by Simone Weil Davis, and it's called *Living Up to the Ads: Gender Fictions of the 1920s*. Although this book ended up being not directly useful to me, I learned from it anyway, and it could come in handy for another project.

From these works, I learn a lot about family and domestic life and how it was perceived in twentieth-century America. It's fascinating stuff, things I had no idea about! For instance, did you know that "[i]n 1900, the typical woman spent 44 hours a week preparing meals and cleaning up after them" and that laundry took all day to do by hand. "By 1975, household food preparation and cleanup had dropped to 10 hours per week, and, by the end of the century, some women spent no time at all on food preparation" and laundry was done by machines (Coleman et al. 52). Refrigeration changed how families were fed because food, including pre-prepared foods such as frozen dinners, could be stored for longer periods of time. The refrigerator changed the work of housewives: they cooked less and shopped more (Coleman et al. 56). By 1934, in a middle- or upper-middle-class home, there would have been several labor-saving devices, such as a vacuum cleaner, an automatic sewing machine, and an electric rather than solid-fuel stove, and many ready-made products would have been available. All these were helpful to homemakers, but they also led to changes in their lives: with less to do, they had less need for hired help and less cause to do things together (such as bread making or rug beating). So social life changed with changes in technology.

In 1929, the Great Depression started, and, at its worst, one-third of the workforce was unemployed. The consequences to family life were devastating; people without jobs were poor, unhealthy, and unhappy. They forestalled marriage and having children, and they moved to places that they thought might offer better luck in the job market. Men left their families to try to find work, and women went into factory jobs that kept them at work for long hours in sometimes dangerous conditions: "the deep economic downturn was also a crisis of the family" (A. Carlson 65). The government stepped in, and its policies emphasized a certain form of the family that hadn't always been the norm (A. Carlson 65). In order to ensure that families had a living wage, and on the presumptions that men made more money for their work than did women and that families (husbands and children) were better cared for by wives and mothers who were full-time homemakers, support programs and the advertising that went with them emphasized the kind of family we now think of as traditional: a husband or father who works outside the home and a wife or mother who works within the home, raising children, preparing food, and keeping everything clean (A. Carlson 64).

So the people at the center of Williams's poem were living in a society that was under stress. The form of the family, the roles of husband and wife, and marital and community relationships were all experiencing change, were all under pressure for broader social and economic reasons. With changes in the home (such as vacuum cleaners and washing machines) that increased the solitude of individuals and couples, especially in an upper-middle-class setting such as that enjoyed by the Williams family, husbands and wives were discovering and experimenting with new ways of communicating and with new forms of intimacy and companionship. In *Images of Family Life in Magazine Advertising, 1920–1978*, Bruce W. Brown says there was a steady rise in the depiction of intimacy between family members in the medium and period he studied (75) and that there was just as steady a decrease in the depiction of wives doing housework with newly available appliances and equipment (31).

What does all this have to do with "This Is Just To Say"? The speaker and the listener in the poem have an "icebox" rather than a refrigerator, which was normal for the period although refrigerators were available. But it means that, in the domestic scene referred to in the poem, the woman probably spent a lot of time handling food, buying it, storing it, preparing it, and cleaning up after meals. In this world, a woman's relationship with food was part of her identity, part of her role in the household and in the marriage. The speaker's transgression, for which he asks forgiveness, has involved a foray into her territory, into the "icebox," and the plundering of her stores, the "plums." But the speaker does not seem to expect to be punished really. Although he acknowledges her territorial privileges over the plums, he emphasizes two other things in their relationship: the enjoyment of sensual experience ("delicious," "so sweet," "so cold") and the act of communicating about that experience, about each other's feelings, about each other's work in the household. The speaker has gently mocked the kind of relationship in which the woman controls the food and the man is there to eat it; he has refigured their marriage as a relationship of intimates, within which they communicate feelings, pleasures, and affection. (Floss's response in "Reply"—which was crafted by Williams and not his wife, we must remember—seems to reject the initiative, doesn't it [Williams, Collected Poems 536]?)

Read in relation to the historical backdrop, in which the material conditions and social understanding of marriage and family life were changing rapidly, the poem appears to challenge older ideas about marriage and to embrace new ideas that emphasize shared intimacy, communication, and affectionate companionship. At the same time, the poem makes what we can read as a social phenomenon intensely personal. Perhaps we can come to a conclusion about the relationship between the social and the personal—that feelings are always intensely personal, even when they are supported by a social context that validates and encourages them. And perhaps we get a glimmer of another idea—that lyric poetry is one of the best ways we have of knowing about this connection between the personal and the social, as this poetry is always written in context but always from a personal point of view.

CONCLUSION

My research in social and historical contexts for "This Is Just To Say" has given me a few more ideas to add to my list.

1. For a woman in 1934, domestic life was labor-intensive, although less so than it had been (Coleman et al. 52).
2. The wife was more isolated in the home than she had been in previous eras, when extended family and employees might have shared the house (Coleman et al. 56).
3. Food was an important part of women's lives (Coleman et al. 52). The refrigerator changed the pattern of housewives' lives: they cooked less and shopped more (Coleman et al. 56).
4. In the period when the poem was written, there was ideological support for the nuclear family (A. Carlson 64), which led to pressure on marriage to be a more intimate and personally rewarding relationship than it had been before (Brown 75, 31).

These pieces of information make me think that, read in relation to the historical backdrop, the poem seems to challenge older ideas about marriage and to embrace new ideas that emphasize shared intimacy, communication, and affectionate companionship. I'll write that down in my "great ideas" file and keep going. You can see how I incorporated some information on social and historical contexts in Sample Essay Two (pp. 177–87).

Social and historical contexts can illuminate works of literature in many ways. We can use them to make our observations about literature more precise and more profound. Knowing more about the domestic and family life of people in the 1930s helps us to see more exactly the qualities of the relationship depicted in the poem: they stand out in contrast much more clearly, now that we know something about the background. Social and historical contexts must always be tied directly to the poem itself; it's not enough to know that things were going on in a general way at the time the poem was written. I'm writing this, for example, during the COVID-19 pandemic, and during the run-up to the 2020 US election; both of these things are weighing on me and affecting my daily life. But they don't really have much to do with what I'm writing here. In our work about "This Is Just To Say," we didn't bother to follow up on biographical details about Williams's life or on historical topics about his time that weren't referred to in the poem. And we also need to stick close to the poem so that we don't commit a biographical fallacy and imagine that we see the poet himself in its lines rather than his invented persona, who is actually speaking in the poem. But handled as evidence, information about social and historical contexts can greatly enrich our analysis of literary works. And we can learn plenty along the way. Forty-four hours a week! Good grief!

REVIEW QUESTIONS

1. How can we narrow the social context of a work of literature to useful topics?
2. How can biographies be useful in identifying contexts that are relevant to the study of literature?
3. What is the biographical fallacy?
4. Why do we read a lot more than we can use when we are doing research?
5. How many times do you think you would read "This Is Just To Say" if you were writing an essay about it? Why do we reread so often in literary studies?

CHAPTER FIVE

Research about the Current Critical Assessment of Literary Works

YOU WILL SOMETIMES BE ASKED TO REFER TO "SECONDARY sources" in your essays, which usually means critical essays and books. Critical essays and books are written by professionals in the field of literary studies. They may be professors or instructors, they may be graduate students (especially doctoral students), or they may be independent scholars. Whatever their occupation, they have been trained as researchers and writers. If they hold doctorate degrees, they've ten years or more studying at college or university (or a combination of the two). An article can take years to develop and publish; a book much longer than that. Articles and books usually go through a long process of revision and improvement, and their publication is acknowledgment of their excellence. Having an essay published in a scholarly journal is like having a painting chosen for a major exhibition, getting an award for best performance at work or at school, or earning a medal in an athletic competition. It's tough to do, and it takes years of practice and a fair amount of talent to pull off.

Good critical writing both acknowledges the critical history to which it belongs and distinguishes itself from that history. In other words, the best critiques build upon past criticism but offer fresh insights and new perspectives. Critical essays and books will devote a lot of space to establishing the relationship between the new ideas and the old ones. In consequence, quite a bit of the material in critical essays and books will be concerned with things that are not familiar to you—and, to be truthful, that you might not find very illuminating. And the technical vocabulary of literary studies may also be a foreign language to you, as literary theory freely imports terms from other languages, especially Greek, Latin, French, and German. The terminology of literary theory also borrows from philosophy, neuroscience, psychology and psychoanalysis, history, sociology, feminism, gender studies, political theory, postcolonial studies, game theory, linguistics, rhetoric ... the list is endless. It's no surprise, then, that you might find reading and using critical essays and books challenging, that you might feel as if the works of literary criticism you try to read are part of a universe to which you do not belong (and may not even want to visit!).

As in other disciplines, the specialized vocabulary and discursive density of literary criticism are necessary features of the ways in which people with advanced knowledge and professional responsibilities talk about things. Medical researchers, for instance, don't talk in plain, ordinary language: they speak of the many systems in the human body, and they use disciplinary vocabulary to describe phenomena and treatment. They have to: it wouldn't be helpful to your orthopedic surgeon to read the instructions, "If the patient's leg hurts, try cutting into it and getting at the problem." It wouldn't help your leg much either. We trust medical professionals to know what they are doing when they talk the way they do; we should also trust that humanities professionals know what they are doing when they use language that most people wouldn't recognize and talk about things that most people have never heard of. They have important work to do, decoding the record of human experience as it is contained in literature, and they've developed ways to make their communication most efficient and precise.

You are not expected to be able to understand this discourse fully or to be able to use its terms comfortably, in the way that professional critics do. But you can get a start: before you finish your undergraduate or college degree, you should have some exposure to the language, the methodologies, and the discoveries of the professional discourse of English studies. If your instructor expects you to do so, then they are prepared to support you in your efforts. Don't be afraid to ask for help. The aim of this chapter is not to replace the support your instructors and librarians can give but to offer a few strategies that will help you to identify and locate useful critical works, read them constructively, and use them as evidence in your own essays.

FINDING CRITICAL WORKS

Assessing Publications

Professional academics in the humanities publish their findings in journals and books. The most valuable of these, for both the scholarly writer and reader, are what are called "peer-reviewed" works. This means that the article or book undergoes a process of assessment by other professionals in the field before it can be accepted for publication. Typically, publications in peer-reviewed journals are double-blind refereed, which means that the name of the author is removed from the manuscript and the names of the "readers" or peer reviewers are not revealed to the author. The work is evaluated according to its merit and not on the basis of personal relationships or status. Normally, reviewers are asked to assess the originality of the findings; the quality of the scholarship, including the review of past work relevant to the topic; the importance of the findings and the areas of knowledge to which they contribute; and, finally, the quality of the writing. You can find out whether a journal is peer reviewed by looking at its website and investigating its "submission guidelines"; the example in the text box will tell you more. Books are a little bit harder to assess, but, normally, anything published by a university press or by a trade publisher that publishes a lot of academic work will also be of the best quality.

Though peer-reviewed material is now widely available on the Internet, much of the material found in a web search will not be peer reviewed. Peer-reviewed works online will be intermingled with a lot of material of more dubious quality. Some of these online offerings might well be valuable and intelligent, but many of them will not be, and some could have very bad information that might well ruin your good efforts. You should trust your library and its catalogues and resources before you trust material from the larger infosphere when you are looking for literary criticism. The library employs people to sift out the best and make it available to you. And, with so many electronic resources available through the library, it's almost as convenient (and less likely to backfire) if you get your sources through the library rather than through other means.

THE SCHOLARLY JOURNAL

The William Carlos Williams Review *is a journal devoted to the poet's work. It has a website that gives information about the journal, how to subscribe, and how to submit works to it. Under "Submission Guidelines," the editor writes, "The author's name should only appear on the cover sheet as the manuscript must be anonymous, with no reference to the author appearing in the text." This information means that the "refereeing" is blind. The members of the Editorial Board for each issue are also listed, and they are experts in the area. These details mean that* The William Carlos Williams Review *is a peer-reviewed journal, and they are guarantees of the quality and suitability of the content for students of literature, and especially for students of Williams's work.*

Using Bibliographies

A bibliography is a collection of references to scholarship. There are thousands of bibliographies in print, and most are now available in electronic form. For work in English studies, the main bibliography is the *Modern Language Association International Bibliography*, which should be available to you through your library's website. Now electronic, the MLA *International Bibliography* has been collecting and organizing references to publications in the area of language and literary study since 1926. Annually, it indexes more than 6,000 journals and book series published by a huge number of publishers. The search interface has been developed over many years and is very sophisticated and fine-grained; each entry is extensively tagged or labeled to allow for complex searches involving many terms. The interface for the *MLAIB* conveniently separates the search returns into types of publication, including "peer-reviewed journals," "books," and "chapters in books." This categorization will help you select high-quality resources.

"I'M HERE TO HELP YOU": YOUR LIBRARIAN

There are other bibliographies that are available in electronic interfaces, and your library will have subscriptions to many of these. Librarians are great resource people, and you should take advantage of the services they offer. They can let you know if the World Shakespeare Bibliography *or* ITER: Gateway to the Middle Ages and the Renaissance, *as examples, would be useful to you. And they can help you figure out how to use these and other databases.*

One of the challenges in using a database like the *MLAIB*, which has millions of unique and complex items in it, is to construct your search so that you collect enough—but not too many—references to works that are relevant to your project. One thing to do is to remember that you are building an argument that you've already started to assemble; you have plenty of evidence already from your reading of the primary material and from your reading in reference works. (You should never use a search of secondary sources to identify a topic; you must be led by what you already know.) I reread "This Is Just To Say," and I review my notes, so as to be sure I will build on my previous research. I'm reminded that my interests include the domestic setting of the poem, the intimacy of the communication, the marital situation, and how the writing expresses those things. I'll try to work these topics into my searches.

I start by looking for items about the work I am centrally concerned with. When I search for "This Is Just To Say" in "anywhere" I get only a handful of "hits"—only nine in total—and only five of these are to articles in "peer-reviewed journals"; none is a book. When I look at the list of "peer-reviewed journal" entries, only one of these seems interesting to me. It's an article by Charles Altieri published in a journal called *Critical Inquiry*. As the interface for the MLAIB allows me to save items that I select, I'll check this one off and get back to it later. I've got to try a broader search so that I can retrieve more references that are going to help me. Now I'll try "William Carlos Williams" (without quotation marks), "anywhere." This search results in too many items: 946 in total and 383 of these in peer-reviewed journals. I have to find a way to narrow this search without missing important items that might be relevant to my interest in "This Is Just To Say."

JOURNALS OR BOOKS?

Because peer-reviewed journals are often available online and because they are shorter than books, they can be easier to handle as research resources. By all means, use them. But if you find that they refer to key books on your topic or that you don't have as much evidence as you'd like from secondary sources using just articles, go back to the MLAIB and begin to go through the books listed in your search results.

There are various ways to narrow your search. As we discussed in the last chapter, you can use Boolean operators to restrict your search results to items in which two or more areas of interest appear. You can limit by giving further particulars about the genre you are interested in ("poetry," for example), by describing an additional topic you are interested in ("women" or "modernism"), or by date of publication, sometimes referred to as "date range." I find "date range" particularly useful; I will often limit my search to the last ten years of publications. If I can find a few items in that list that concern my interests, they will refer me to works published in the past that might also be of interest to me. This is one of the advantages of the requirement in professional scholarship that the author acknowledge where his or her argument sits in relation to what has been said on the topic before.

My initial search for "William Carlos Williams" returned many more items than I could possibly look through. I tried various ways of narrowing the search while still leaving me with enough items for a solid research base. I tried narrowing the date range to "2000" to the present, which reduced the number of items listed to 135 in total, of which 69 were peer-reviewed articles and 17 were books. On my "to do" list, I added two of these books and six articles. Then I checked on the availability of these works. The books are in my library, and several of the articles are available in the print journals collection. Five articles are available electronically; as I'm working at home, I'll try those first. If I need to do more research after that, I'll continue with a day at the library in the coming week.

SEARCH TIPS

You are seeking search results that will be relevant to your interests and manageable in terms of volume.

- *Begin with a search specific to your interests.*
- *If that doesn't work, do a very broad search.*
- *Narrow with a Boolean operator such as AND or by date range.*
- *Follow up on works that are cited within articles and books that you find helpful, if you feel you need to do more research.*

Students often ask how many secondary sources they should use. Your instructor may have a different answer than I give to that question, so ask your instructor if they haven't already specified. Your instructor might want you to become more familiar with literary critical discourse and may require that you read and refer to three or four articles, for instance. When I am asked this question, what I usually say is this: "Use as many as you need to make the argument you want to make." You may get all you need from a couple of articles, the *OED*, and an encyclopedia or two. You may need to use more sources in order to make your argument, and you will certainly need to read more than you use. But keep in mind that the objective of the essay is to offer a strong, deep, and sharp argument, so measure your research efforts by whether they have helped you meet that goal. If they haven't, do more. If they have, you can probably stop there.

USING YOUR LIBRARY'S ASSETS

My library has a service that allows me to print or email my marked list. Before or after printing or emailing, I can turn the references (or citations, as they are often called) into a list that is formatted in the form I want for my list of "Works Cited" or my "Bibliography," whichever my instructor (which in this case is me!) has asked for. Although the results must be checked carefully, this step can save me a few minutes and make sure that I have all the information I need to submit with my essay.

READING CRITICAL WORKS

When you read critical works, you are looking for further evidence for the essay you are working on. Focus on finding information that will help you in one or more of the following ways:

1. It will confirm and strengthen the ideas, feelings, and insights you have already had.
2. It will enhance or supplement the ideas, feelings, and insights you have already had.
3. It will give you new knowledge and may correct misunderstandings or challenge perceptions you have already had.
4. It will help you stage the argument that you will make in your essay.
5. It can help you challenge ideas that you don't find persuasive in order to strengthen your own argument.

You will learn more about the practice of literary criticism and the methods of literary theory as you read, but don't get hung up on trying to figure out every term or reference. Certainly, these details are important, but you do not have time for them at the moment.

The time to decide to devote your life to literary theory and literary criticism hasn't yet arrived; when it does, you will be ready! For now, you have a deadline to meet and an assignment to complete.

Typically, you will want to skim through articles, even just the first few pages and perhaps the conclusion, before you decide which to read more carefully. You can be mistaken, as I was when I started "Presence and Reference in a Literary Text: The Example of Williams' 'This Is Just to Say'" by Charles Altieri. On the first page I saw the names "Aristotle," "Derrida," and "Wittgenstein" (and not Williams); I thought, "This article is more about theory than it is about Williams, and I'm not sure it's going to be very useful. And I don't have time to reread Aristotle, Derrida, and Wittgenstein: I have a deadline, after all." A good rule is to be wary of literary criticism that assumes you are on a "last-name-only" basis with major theorists of the last 2,500 years, as if you were at boarding school or summer camp with them! I'm kidding, but I'm also serious: much of the literary criticism of the last quarter of the twentieth century was as much about theory as it was about literature. But—a word of warning!—in this case I was wrong: I returned to the Altieri article later, as so many other articles that I read referred to it that I thought I must have misjudged it. And indeed I had. (Confessing to one's mistakes and oversights is a pleasure often granted the researcher.)

When I read the Altieri article more thoroughly, I found that the last ten pages of the article were devoted to a close reading of "This Is Just To Say." Altieri has some very good points to make that help me identify ways in which the poem's style makes the poem seem more intimate. For instance, he points out that "This" in the title is a deictic, a word that points to something and depends on context for meaning, as if we can all see "this" thing, as if we are in the same small space. Altieri also helped me clarify and extend my sense of the nature of the speaker's apology. Altieri writes, "The justness of the speaker's note is its recognition of his weakness and its lovely combination of self-understanding with an implicit faith in his wife's capacity to understand and accept his deed and, beyond that, to comprehend his human existence as a balance of weakness, self-knowledge, and concern" (501). In one sentence, Altieri has connected the language of the poem with the intimacy and love that I detected in it. I can use this statement, and others by Altieri, to confirm my sense of the poem and to enhance and supplement my comments about those topics.

After reading the five articles on my list, I have decided that two (by Bob Johnson and Daniel Morris), while interesting, are not relevant to my essay. Johnson's article is about politics, and Morris's is about homoeroticism and the visual arts in Williams's work. The other three are relevant, and I take extensive notes from each of them. Like Altieri's, Celia Carlson's article helps me sharpen and clarify the feelings and ideas I already had. She writes, for instance, that "Objects in Williams's poems, far from being 'innocent' arte-facts in the world, demonstrate the quality of Williams's relations with himself and his others" (C. Carlson 27), which will help me write about the plums and the icebox. Theodora Graham's article is the most interesting to me, and I read it carefully and thoroughly. It is centrally concerned with Williams's representation in his writing of marriage in general and of his marriage in particular. Graham puts her finger on something I had sensed but wasn't sure how to articulate: "wherever she [the speaker's wife] appears, the writing is not *about* her but about her relation to him" (Graham 170). By and large, according to Graham, Williams's writing reflects his convic-tion that marriage was both what kept him grounded in the present and the material and what prevented him from fulfilling himself as a writer and genius. "In the drama of their life together, one of the most compelling stories he knew, Williams portrayed himself as the tormented artist, repeatedly tempted to overthrow his conven-tional life—represented by Flossie—and repeatedly retreating into the familiar and certain still center she provided" (Graham 170). Graham's article supports my previous insights, extends them, and offers me new information gained from her extensive knowledge of Williams's work and biography. (For instance, I wasn't aware that Williams was frequently unfaithful to his wife and that his struggles around this fact are one of the topics of his verse.)

All three articles contribute to how I might be able to stage my argument. Each says, explicitly or implicitly, that the relationship between men and women, especially the marital relationship, is one of the enduring, even obsessive concerns in Williams's work. The authors of these articles do not entirely agree: Carlson leans toward criticizing Williams for objectifying women (although she is generous and thoughtful in her appraisal); Graham portrays the poet's feelings and ideas about women as the grounds for tremendous personal and artistic struggle; Altieri sees a much more peaceful heart at the center of the domestic scene than do the others. I can characterize this collection of views in such a way that can help me stage what I want to say. I might write, for instance, that critics do not entirely agree and briefly describe these three views. Then I could say that I would like to measure "This Is Just To Say" in relation to the poles these critics have established. Recalling the historical and social research that I have done, I think I can add that to the reading with some background information about the era in which the poem was written.

I am satisfied that the research I've done in the secondary sources is sufficient for my essay. I know the essays I've read are good quality, and I believe I've got a fairly representative sample of critical opinion on the topics that interest me—although I know my research hasn't been exhaustive. (If I were writing for publication, I would have to make sure that my research was exactly that: exhaustively exhaustive, thoroughly thorough, completely complete! But, as a student, you are not writing for publication.) I may find when I go to pull the essay together that there are some bits and pieces missing in the architecture. If that's the case, I can return to my notes and to the list of references I collected in my search process. If I need to check a few additional things then, I will be able to. For now, though, I'm ready to move on to organizing my evidence and starting to build my argument.

TAKING NOTES FROM CRITICAL READINGS

Let's remember that most of the time you spend working on an essay should be spent in doing and organizing the research. If you spend the time doing that, you will save time writing and make the last part of the essay preparation the easiest and most satisfying. Careful notes from your secondary sources will help.

As soon as I decide I am going to skim a critical essay or book, I make sure I have all the bibliographic information, and I open a file with that information at the top. I name the file with the topic and the last name of the author of the essay or book (e.g., "Williams_altieri.doc").

I find this is a good way to keep track of my notes, but you may have other ways of handling your files. Whatever you do, be consistent and thorough. There is just about nothing worse in the course of writing an essay than having to track down a quotation or an idea that you've neglected to write down or properly document in your notes.

In my notes, I try to put a summary of the argument or field of the essay at the top, unless that is evident from the title. This can be very brief (say "feminism plus biography, reading of Williams's poetry, comparing early and late"); it's just to remind me of the work and to help me decide later if it's useful to go back to it or if it's the source of the quotation I'm looking for. I then copy out quotations that interest me, just as I noted evidence from the poem itself. I try not to decide beforehand how I'm going to use the quotation, although, by this point, my selections are starting to be made on the basis of my ideas about the literature I am studying. I copy them out, rather than using shortcuts to copy and paste, for two reasons. One is that I believe firmly that copying them out helps me to look at each word and understand them better. Two is that I don't want to bring in a huge amount of material that will take a long time to go over; copying and pasting encourages quantity over quality, and I will regret that later. You do what you like, but I am always glad that I've taken the time to make careful notes. I type very quickly, though; there is that to consider.

MANAGING YOUR TIME WHEN WRITING ESSAYS

There's no great shortcut to the writing of good essays. I find that the easiest way to think about the long road to the finished essay is to understand that you are really trying to learn in the process and to produce something special for your reader; those things take time. A great speech, a beautiful painting, a super computer program—none of these is made overnight. Generally speaking, I think you should count on a full day's work for every page of the essay. I would divide that roughly into one-third reading and rereading of the primary text or texts, one-third other reading, and one-third writing time.

I try to label each quotation with something that will cue me to its main point later, again for my review of the notes. In the case of the essay I'm developing about the Williams poem, I might label the notes "intimacy," "woman/wife," "style," and so on, loosely reflecting the categories that I began to develop when I did my first close reading of the poem and that I further expanded when I read around in reference works and social and historical materials. I do all this so that, when I come to organize my evidence, I can make easy matches between the primary and secondary materials, between the poem and the critical statements that apply to it.

I also take notes in my list of great ideas, which is really growing. I'm looking forward to reading it over and getting that warm, happy feeling I get from seeing how smart I really am! I'm joking—but you will probably be pleasantly surprised when you look over your list. It's a general rule that we are smarter over time than we are in the moment, so the record of your insights will be richer and broader than what you think right now about the same things.

Here is a list of reflections I've had as a result of my critical reading; I will add these to my list of great ideas:

1. There is support in the criticism for my idea that marriage is a central concern of "This Is Just To Say." Critics also claim that marriage and fidelity are enduring concerns of Williams's poetry as a whole (Altieri 500-01; Graham 163, 170).

2. There is some critical disagreement about Williams's ideas about women. I may be able to situate my perception of the representation in "This Is Just To Say" of the woman and the speaker's relationship to her in relation to this range of views (Altieri 501; C. Carlson 27; Graham 164–66).

3. One critic (C. Carlson) says that objects in Williams's poems represent Williams's feelings about himself and others. So the "plums" are plums, but they might also be used to express and focus the speaker's feelings, or the feelings between the speaker and another person pictured in the poem (C. Carlson 27).

4. Celia Carlson also says that there is critical interest in how sensuousness is expressed in poetry and that "much

of Williams's energy in his lyric poetry comes from his attempts to harness what he viewed in rather traditional terms as the feminine power of the body" (27).

5. Critics generally reinforce my sense that the language choices are what give the impression of intimacy and materiality (Altieri 499–500).

You can now review Sample Essay Three (pp. 189–201) to see how I incorporated critical works into my essay on the poem.

CONCLUSION

Reading literary criticism written by professionals is hard. You are not expected to be fluent in the languages of literary theory or to chat easily about the critical history of works that you are studying. What you may be expected to do is to read selected works of criticism, grasp something of their arguments, and isolate statements that can be used as evidence to support your argument in your essay. Seek out refereed articles and books published by university presses; use the resources made available through your library, including the catalogue, bibliographies, and works themselves; construct searches so as to produce enough relevant results but not too many to handle. Focus on collecting evidence that will confirm, enhance, challenge, or correct your ideas and feelings and that will help you stage your argument. Ask questions of your instructors and your librarians, use your library's tools, and take careful notes. Give yourself enough time to understand what you read and to reflect on the ideas you are collecting. Most of all, don't panic: do the best you can. Do it carefully and honestly, and the results will be good. In fact, I wager the results will be better than you expected. And you may even like criticism which, as arcane and baroque as it may sometimes seem, is comprised of the best efforts of great minds to work carefully and honestly through the reasons that literature does what it does to us—it changes our minds, moves our hearts, and opens our speech to new words, new concepts, and new ways of being.

REVIEW QUESTIONS

1. Why is literary criticism often hard to understand?
2. What are some techniques to use to narrow a search in a large database?
3. What does a "double-blind peer-review" process mean?
4. Why are works available on the web not as reliable as ones available through your library?
5. What should you use secondary sources for?

CHAPTER SIX

Inventing Your Argument

ESSAYS IN ENGLISH STUDIES ARE ARGUMENTS ABOUT THE meaning, power, or structure of works of literature. By "argument," I mean the definition given in the *OED*: "A connected series of statements or reasons intended to establish a position (and, *hence*, to refute the opposite); a process of reasoning." Arguments in English studies present an interpretation based on evidence. The interpretation is logically organized so as to persuade the reader of its strength. Implicitly or explicitly, the author acknowledges that this argument is not the only possible one about a topic. Detectives and scientists always seek the best possible explanation for the phenomena that they analyze, but they know that there may be other plausible explanations. Literary works are so complex that there is no single "right" answer about their meaning, why they are powerful and in what ways, or how they are built so as to produce those meanings and those effects. But there are stronger and weaker arguments, and your essay will be judged on the strength of its argument.

Professional literary critics have to produce arguments that are original—that have never been made before. You don't have to do that. What you have to do is produce arguments from your unique perspective, arguments that accurately reflect the material you are working on, that make sense, that interest the reader, and that tell them something they might not have thought of before. You can imagine your reader as an accomplished, hard-working, engaged student such as yourself: work to persuade and impress that reader with your artful argument and your command of evidence. Imagine yourself also open to their questions and objections; imagining a different point of view will improve your argument. But imagine also the satisfaction you both will feel in having shared some good ideas, supported precisely by evidence, about something about which you have common experience.

We've worked hard on gathering evidence, which is the best guarantee of a strong argument. Now we need to know more about how to organize that evidence, make statements about it, connect those statements, and communicate their importance to our understanding of the work of literature with which the essay is concerned. After that, we'll put on the finishing touches: making sure the structure of the argument is perfect, checking the grammar and spelling, preparing the list of works cited, and confirming that the presentation is just right.

ARRANGING YOUR EVIDENCE

Reviewing Your Labeled Evidence

Throughout this book, I have emphasized working from evidence to argument, rather than the other way around. You will learn more this way, and your essay will be stronger and more interesting. If you have been working with the methods outlined in this book, you have collected evidence from at least two sources: your first impressions and your close reading of the work of literature itself. You may also have collected evidence from these sources:

- other works by the same author;
- other works by authors contemporary with the one you are researching;

- the introduction and annotations to scholarly editions;
- biographies and biographical articles in reference works;
- dictionaries, especially the *Oxford English Dictionary*;
- encyclopedias, including specialized ones devoted to literature or culture in the national and temporal realms of the work you are studying;
- works about the social and historical contexts of the literature; and
- critical essays and books.

In each case, I've asked you to label your evidence. Let's consider, for a moment, our evidence gathering for the essay on "This Is Just To Say." The labels attached to quotations from the poem relate your perceptions of the meaning, power, and structure of the work to the parts of the poem that provoked those perceptions. The labels on quotations from your other reading connect these quotations to your ideas, both original and developing. This evidence and these labels will help take you from your first impressions to the argument that will comprise your essay. Your essay will therefore be neatly and firmly connected to you—the writer—and to the material the essay is about—the literature. Here's how to proceed.

Categorizing Your Evidence

It's time to go back and read your evidence—all of it—again. Review your list of first impressions and your quotations from the poem, from reference works, from works about social and historical contexts, and from any critical works you've read that you found useful. These are the building blocks of your essay; if they are strong, chances are the essay will also be strong. So assess whether you've got a pile of good bricks. If you have, the next task is to fit them together into a form that is functional and pleasing. That's what the next process is about.

Look at the labels you've assigned to the evidence. You may have 15 or 20 or even more different labels; you probably want 4, 5, or 6, in the end. If some overlap or duplicate others, merge them together. If some of the evidence doesn't fit in the new categories, then set it aside; it may not have a place in this essay.

In my work on "This Is Just To Say," I've got a lot of labels:

- food
- sensual pleasure
- communication
- intimacy
- naughtiness
- poet/persona/recipient of the note (identification?)
- definite articles
- verb tense
- imperative mood
- deictics
- material world
- everyday language (Anglo-Saxon?)
- visual word
- transgression?
- eroticism
- marriage
- the feminine
- domesticity
- marriage in society
- Flossie as wife in poems
- Williams and marriage
- things and relations

I need to reduce the number of categories I have here. Roughly speaking, I'm looking to have one category for each of the subtopics in my essay. Here I'll reduce my categories to five, into which I can slot most of my labeled items:

1. LANGUAGE (communications, poet/persona, everyday language, definite articles, deictics, verb tense)
2. MATERIAL REALITY (food, domesticity, things and relations)
3. MARRIAGE (marriage in society, Flossie as wife, Williams and marriage)
4. SENSUOUSNESS (sensual pleasure, visual word)
5. EMOTION (intimacy, naughtiness, transgression, imperative mood)

I'm still not sure what my argument (my little brick shed, if you will allow me to work this metaphor a little) is going to be, but things are beginning to take shape. You'll notice I have made some judgment calls, and they indicate how my mind is starting to shape the argument. I've put "visual word" under "sensuousness" rather than under "language," for instance, because I'm specifically interested in the evocative, sensual effects of "plums." After doing this, I realize that I can probably move all of the language items into the other categories, bringing my categories down to four. I like this move, in part because it balances things out and in part because it will strengthen the evidence I have in each category, as I will have a piece of linguistic evidence for each topic: this suits the study of literature, which, after all, is made of language. So my recast list is as follows:

1. MATERIAL REALITY (food, domesticity, things and relations, *everyday language, deictics, verb tense*)
2. MARRIAGE (marriage in society, Flossie as wife, Williams and marriage, *poet/persona*)
3. SENSUOUSNESS (sensual pleasure, visual word, *definite articles*)
4. EMOTION (intimacy, naughtiness, transgression, imperative mood, *communications*)

Now my categories are balanced, each having about the same number of items in it.

FIRST IMPRESSIONS, REVIEWED

My first impressions, from my close reading of the poem, were as follows:

1. *"This Is Just To Say" is about sensual, moral, and interpersonal experience in the material, everyday world.*
2. *"This Is Just To Say" is about relationships between people and about how these relationships are shaped by the use of language.*
3. *"This Is Just To Say" is about poetry and how it is different or the same as everyday acts of communication.*

When I review my first impressions (consult the text box), I see that they have been strengthened, enriched, and supplemented by my research, and I know that the combination of gut response or first impressions and the more textured, nuanced, and detailed observations that have come through my reading outside of the poem will make for a good essay: I will be writing about what I believe and feel, but I will be doing so in a logical, objective fashion. It's this combination that the process of reading and rereading that I have emphasized produces, and it is a process that will make the writing of the essay as easy as it can be. This process reflects the combination of the subjective element (you, the researcher and essay writer) and the object of your investigation (the work of literature), a combination that I describe in Chapter One and that forms the foundation of all essays about literature.

Charting Your Evidence

I will now arrange my evidence in these categories. Typically, I actually make a chart or table, either using my word processor or on a large sheet of paper. (I have special huge graph paper just for this purpose! But that's just one of my idiosyncrasies; I love graph paper. I have colored pencils and markers that I use to make the charts. I tape them up on the wall above my desk, so that, when I'm writing, I can refer to them.) You could just head a file with each category and cut and paste into that file all of the evidence you have collected that belongs in that category; then you will be able to reorder the evidence as your argument begins to take shape. You can bring these categories together in one file after you've made separate files for each category, or you can keep the category files separate and use another file to bring pieces together as you need them. Using computer files to arrange your categorized evidence is probably more efficient than making a chart on graph paper, which takes time and can get messy with reorganizing. Some people like to use brainstorming software or textual databases (you can use spreadsheet programs to make textual databases). Some like moving around sheets of paper, highlighting in different colors, or using categorized index cards arranged in piles around the room. Whatever works for you—the important thing is to line up your evidence in categories.

The charts I've prepared for this chapter are abbreviated; in your own, you could put whole quotations or paraphrases, and you must make sure that you have attached to your categorized evidence the information about the sources you've used because you'll need to document your references. (In my charting of evidence from the poem, for example, I've put line numbers beside each bit taken from "This Is Just To Say.") Once you're finished your chart, you will have a map of your essay, and you'll be able to work from the map to find your way home.

First Version of My Chart: Evidence from Poem

	MATERIAL REALITY	MARRIAGE	SENSUOUSNESS	EMOTION
Poem	"*the* plums" 2 "*the* icebox" 4 "breakfast" 8 "that" 3, "which" 5 (deictics)	Title "I/me," "you" "icebox" 4 "breakfast" 8 (domesticity) "you were probably saving" 6-7	"I have eaten" 1 "delicious" 10 "sweet" 11 "cold" 12	Title "I/me," "you" "Forgive me" 9

That's a good start. Now I'll look over my findings from the reference works. This is what I observe after reading them through.

1. From the dictionary, I learned (or was reminded) that a plum is both a fruit and a color.
2. From the dictionary, I learned that most of the words used in the poem derive from Old English and are older and simpler words compared to others in modern English.
3. From the scholarly edition, I confirmed that Williams wrote the poem as if it were a note to his wife, that he wrote it in 1934, and that, later, he wrote a "Reply" to it in her voice.
4. From the biographical article, I learned that Williams was a doctor and a father and that he and Florence were married for decades.

I'll categorize the first observation under "sensuousness," the second under "material reality," and the fourth under "marriage." I'm not sure about the third one. It's definitely about communications, but it's also about marriage. I look back over my longer list of labels, and I see that I've put "communications" under emotion. It seems counter-intuitive not to put the third observation under marriage, but I'm trying to stay disciplined and stick to my categories and what informed them. So I'm going to put the third observation, about the fact that the poem is written in the style of a note, under "emotion" in my chart.

Second Version of My Chart:
Evidence from the Poem and from Reference Works

	MATERIAL REALITY	MARRIAGE	SENSUOUSNESS	EMOTION
Poem	"*the* plums" 2 "*the* icebox" 4 "breakfast" 8 "that" 3, "which" 5 (deictics)	Title "I/me," "you" "icebox" 4 "breakfast" 8 (domesticity) "you were probably saving" 6–7	"I have eaten" 1 "delicious" 10 "sweet" 11 "cold" 12	Title "I/me," "you" "Forgive me" 9
Reference Works	Dictionary: Old English words	Biography: Williams's marriage	Dictionary: plum	Edition: "Reply"

My research into social and historical contexts for "This Is Just To Say" has given me a few more ideas to add to my list.

1. For a woman in 1934, domestic life was labor intensive, although less so than it had been (Coleman et al. 52).
2. The wife was more isolated in the home than she had been in previous eras, when an extended family and employees might have shared the house (Coleman et al. 56).
3. Food was an important part of women's lives (Coleman et al. 52). The refrigerator changed the pattern of housewives' lives: they cooked less and shopped more (Coleman et al. 56).
4. When the poem was written, there was ideological support for the nuclear family (A. Carlson 64), which led to pressure on marriage to be a more intimate and personally rewarding relationship than it had been before (Brown 75, 31).

Looking at my chart, I think I'll put the first and third observations under "material reality," the second under "emotion," and divide the fourth between "marriage" and "sensuousness" (on the basis that intimacy might involve sensuality in one form or another). As you can see, some of the evidence could go under more than one category, and, in the end, I may find a particular piece more useful in a different category. For now, however, I'm not worried about that.

Third Version of My Chart: Adding Evidence about Social Context

	MATERIAL REALITY	MARRIAGE	SENSUOUSNESS	EMOTION
Poem	"*the* plums" 2 "*the* icebox" 4 "breakfast" 8 "that" 3, "which" 5 (deictics)	Title "I/me," "you" "icebox" 4 "breakfast" 8 (domesticity) "you were probably saving" 6–7	"I have eaten" 1 "delicious" 10 "sweet" 11 "cold" 12	Title "I/me," "you" "Forgive me" 9
Reference Works	Dictionary: Old English words	Biography: Williams's marriage	Dictionary: plum	Edition: "Reply"
Social and Historical Contexts	Women's work labor intensive Food an important part of women's lives	Nuclear family	Intimacy in marriage	Wife isolated

Finally, I got some information and support from researching the literary criticism about the poem and about Williams's poetry. I summarized this evidence as follows (although I have files with quotations to draw upon for the actual essay, as I do with the other secondary sources).

1. There is support in the criticism for my idea that marriage is a central concern of "This Is Just To Say." Critics also claim that marriage and fidelity are enduring concerns of Williams's poetry as a whole (Altieri 500–01; Graham 163, 170).

2. There is some critical disagreement about Williams's ideas about women (Altieri 501; C. Carlson 27; Graham 164–66).

3. One critic (C. Carlson) says that objects in Williams's poems represent Williams's feelings about himself and others (C. Carlson 27).

4. Celia Carlson also says that there is critical interest in how sensuousness is expressed in poetry and that "much of Williams's energy in his lyric poetry comes from his attempts to harness what he viewed in rather traditional terms as the feminine power of the body" (27).

5. Critics generally reinforce my sense that the language choices are what give the impression of intimacy and materiality (for example, Altieri 499–500).

I'll put the first and second ones in the "marriage" category, the third in "material reality" and "emotion," and the fourth ... hmmm. The fourth seems to belong in all the categories. I'm going to leave it aside for the moment. You'll notice I've put the third piece of evidence in two categories, which is fine; I'll figure out when I write the essay if it is best in one or the other or if there are a couple of observations on that topic from the criticism that I can divide between the two topics. No worries; we're still brainstorming.

THE EVIDENCE THAT WON'T FIT

Sometimes you have to set aside pieces of evidence if there's no category for them. But sometimes you'll find an observation or a set of observations in a critical work that seems to crystallize what you've been thinking about the poem. If you do, set it aside, as it could come in handy as a way to introduce your topic. In this case, I've been unable to categorize "Critics generally reinforce my sense that the language choices are what give the impression of intimacy and materiality (for example, Altieri 499–500)" because it seems to fall into all my categories. It concurs with my initial impressions, so it does seem to articulate what I've been thinking from the beginning. This is very lucky for me, and I'll hold on to that idea and the quotations that back it up for possible use in my introductory paragraph.

Fourth Version of My Evidence Chart: Adding Evidence from Criticism

	MATERIAL REALITY	MARRIAGE	SENSUOUSNESS	EMOTION
Poem	"*the* plums" 2 "*the* icebox" 4 "breakfast" 8 "that" 3, "which" 5 (deictics)	Title "I/me," "you" "icebox" 4 "breakfast" 8 (domesticity) "you were probably saving" 6–7	"I have eaten" 1 "delicious" 10 "sweet" 11 "cold" 12	Title "I/me," "you" "Forgive me" 9
Reference Works	Dictionary: Old-English words	Biography: Williams's marriage	Dictionary: plum	Edition: "Reply"
Social and Historical Contexts	Women's work labor intensive Food an important part of women's lives	Nuclear family	Intimacy in marriage	Wife isolated
Criticism	Objects and feelings (C. Carlson)	Marriage is cen- tral concern Williams and women?	Poetry and sensuousness and the feminine (C. Carlson)	Feelings and objects (C. Carlson)

I'm happy with this chart. I don't feel there are any gaps in it that desperately need filling. If I did, I would review my files to see if there's something I've overlooked or something that could be moved from one category to another. If there wasn't, then I might go back to the library. But it's not necessary to have all the columns and rows filled; in one section of your argument, social context might provide important evidence that it doesn't in other sections, while, in another section, you might rely on the dictionary more than on criticism. The only thing you *must have in each category is evidence from the works of literature you are studying.*

ALERT!

If you have a category that has no evidence from the primary text(s) (in this case, "This Is Just To Say"), then you need to rethink the categories or get that evidence. That's the only type of evidence that must appear in all the categories. Your essay is, first and foremost, about the literature. So go back to the literary work or works you are writing about or reformulate your categories if you don't have evidence from your primary texts in each category.

CONCLUSION

I'm ready to start writing my essay now, to start composing my argument, which will be "a connected series of statements or reasons intended to establish a position (and, *hence*, to refute the opposite); a process of reasoning." Like any good argument, mine will be based firmly on evidence. The evidence I need is all nicely arranged and ready to be used—I won't be distracted when I am writing it up by a missing page number or a lost quotation from the poem. It's a bit like baking: you're much better off to assemble your ingredients first, make sure there is nothing missing, sort the dry from the wet, let the butter soften, and even measure things out—when you do this preparation, you're ready to mix things up and create that beautiful cake. No need to rush out for vanilla while the egg whites wilt and the oven heats up the kitchen. So we've got everything ready, made sure nothing is missing, and now we just need to assemble the batter and bake our cake. Or rather, I, the essay writer, need to connect the statements and reasons intended to establish my position and to present the whole as the result of a process of reasoning. With icing and sprinkles on top!

REVIEW QUESTIONS

1. Why are there no single "right" answers to questions we have about literary works?
2. What are the key words to remember about what an essay is?
3. How are literary critics similar to detectives and scientists?
4. What kind of evidence is absolutely essential to your essay?
5. What should you do if there are gaps in your evidence chart?

Section Three

COMPOSITION

CHAPTER SEVEN

Composing Your Argument

THIS CHAPTER IS ABOUT WRITING YOUR THESIS STATEMENT, which is the outline of your argument. The thesis statement is a summary of your argument: according to my old friend the *Oxford English Dictionary*, a thesis in logic or composition is a "proposition laid down or stated, especially as a theme to be discussed and proved, or to be maintained against attack." The thesis statement describes the evidence you are using, states your interpretations of this evidence, and brings those insights together into a conclusion that is about the way the literature works, what it means, or how and why it has the emotional impact it does.

Writing the thesis statement is half the burden of writing the essay as a whole. It's hard to do, and you should budget about half your writing time for composing and revising it. It'll be the first and last thing you work on in writing the essay. Apart from its importance in setting out your argument, it is also significant because it sets the first impression for your reader. So it must be written as well as you can write, as clearly, economically, and precisely as possible. Every word must be in the right place, and every place must have the right word. When you have finished your thesis statement, it should remind you of an enameled Easter egg or a rose in bloom or a marvelous fruitcake: a beautiful thing, composed of many parts brought together into a unique way to form a singular and complete form.

INDUCTIVE REASONING

Arguments in literary criticism are instances of what is called *inductive reasoning.* That means they analyze examples in order to come to broader conclusions. If this ice cube is cold and that ice cube is cold, we can conclude that it is likely that ice is cold. If an animal has four legs, fur, and suckles its young, it is probably a mammal and therefore can be grouped and studied with other similar animals. If you and Peter and Imelda all like Margaret Atwood's novels, you are likely to share other interests, and you might want to strike up a friendship. If a novel examines the lives of women in various circumstances, we can argue that it is concerned with the condition of women in the society in which it is set. In all of your essays, your argument should use inductive reasoning to move from particular pieces of evidence to broader generalizations about the work of literature and its meaning, emotional power, and aesthetic value. These generalizations may include statements about the author, about literature in general, about social or historical issues, or about combinations of these things. The important thing is to remember that *induction* means going from the particular to the general, from specific evidence to a general conclusion.

Arguments in literary criticism are *not* examples of *deductive* reasoning. Deductive reasoning moves from general principles to specific qualities. By and large, deductive reasoning is imprecise and often incorrect when applied to phenomena as varied and rich as literature. Here are some examples of deductive reasoning, which proceeds from the general to the particular. If an animal is a mammal, it probably has four legs, fur, and suckles its young; okay, that example works, to a certain extent (whales are mammals without four legs, as are humans, and neither has fur, exactly). If you, Peter, and Imelda are friends, you probably all like the same books; this example is less sturdy, as there are so many different kinds of books and people are so infinitely complex that the conclusion is unlikely, although possible. Another example: literature, taken as a whole, is about truth, beauty, and the human condition; therefore, any individual work of literature is about truth, beauty, and the human condition. This statement is patently not true; there are many works of literature about lies and ugliness, and some are about the perceptions and experiences of non-human creatures. Besides, we don't agree about what constitutes beauty, truth, or the human condition, so the statement begs more questions than it answers, and it can only be meaningful after those questions are resolved.

A great way to get your essay off to a *terrible* start is to make a sweeping statement about literature or about human life and imagine that this generalization somehow sets the stage for particular observations you are going to make about the work you are studying. I warn my students that an opening sentence with the words "since the beginning of time" or "people have always" or "it is universally true" is a dud, so they have to go back to the drawing board. Sometimes they tell me that they've been taught to open their essays this way, and I believe them. But in college or university, we try to argue from the specific to the general—and not the other way around. And that first sentence is the most important sentence of your essay; use it wisely and well.

COMPOSING THE THESIS STATEMENT

Writing the Subtopic Sentences

Please note that some instructors consider the "thesis statement" to be a paragraph or multiple sentences, while others define it as the single sentence that best sums up your argument in the essay. Below, I'll talk about building and refining the opening paragraph of the essay, a section that some of your professors will call the "introduction" and others will call the "thesis statement." The process and goals are the same even if the terminology is different!

Let's remind ourselves that the strength of our arguments will depend on the quality of our evidence and how we present it. So it makes sense to begin with our evidence as we begin to build our thesis statement. I'll review my chart and then write a sentence or two summarizing the contents of each of my categories of evidence. This way, my ideas are tied closely to the full range of evidence that I've collected and included in my chart. Just to remind us of the evidence, here is the fourth version of that chart:

Fourth Version of My Evidence Chart

	MATERIAL REALITY	MARRIAGE	SENSUOUSNESS	EMOTION
Poem	"*the* plums" 2 "*the* icebox" 4 "breakfast" 8 "that" 3, "which" 5 (deictics)	Title "I/me," "you" "icebox" 4 "breakfast" 8 (domesticity) "you were probably saving" 6–7	"I have eaten" 1 "delicious" 10 "sweet" 11 "cold" 12	Title "I/me," "you" "Forgive me" 9
Reference Works	Dictionary: Old-English words	Biography: Williams's marriage	Dictionary: plum	Edition: "Reply"
Social and Historical Contexts	Women's work labor intensive Food an important part of women's lives	Nuclear family	Intimacy in marriage	Wife isolated
Criticism	Objects and feelings (C. Carlson)	Marriage is central concern Williams and women?	Poetry and sensuousness and the feminine (C. Carlson)	Feelings and objects (C. Carlson)

Reading down the columns, I'll summarize the information I have in the chart. I'll write a sentence for each basic idea and use the most precise words I can find.

MATERIAL REALITY: "This Is Just To Say" uses vocabulary and grammatical choices to emphasize the material reality of the scene it evokes. Set in a kitchen, at the locus of women's work in the period in which it was written, it ties the feelings expressed and evoked in the poem to a specific relationship between two people.

MARRIAGE: Marriage and his relationships with women in general are central concerns in the poetry of William Carlos Williams. "This Is Just To Say" is written as if it were an act of communication between the speaker and his spouse.

SENSUOUSNESS: The vocabulary choices in the poem depict the scene as being rich with sensory experience and imply that the relationship between the poem's speaker and the person to whom the poem is addressed is also a sensual one.

EMOTION: The emotions expressed in the poem are profound. At the same time, the mode of communication and the "Reply" that Williams wrote later in the persona of the spouse suggest remoteness and even isolation or alienation between the "writer" of the note and its "reader."

Composing the Body of the Introduction

When I review these sentences, I look for the sentence that most clearly expresses the central topic of my research and ideas. In this case, it's the first sentence about marriage in Williams's poetry. If I select "marriage" as my topic, I can talk about material reality, sensuousness, emotion, the language that expresses these aspects of the poem, and social and biographical contexts—all are related to marriage. If, instead, I decided on "deictics" as my topic, I would have a tough time talking about plums; if I chose "sensuousness," I would have to wriggle around to discuss the icebox and how the kitchen and food were central to women's lives during the period. So I'll put that sentence on marriage first.

DECIDING ON YOUR TOPIC

This isn't the only topic I could take for my essay from the evidence that I've gathered. With some slight rearrangement, I could craft an argument about communication, about poetry and sensuousness, or about how the female is understood in this poem. If I wasn't satisfied that I had a strong topic, I would go back to the evidence, reread it, review my categorization, and see if that helped. If I was really stuck, I would go back to my reading and try to cast the net a bit more widely. I hope by this stage not to have to do that, but, if I have to, I will.

After deciding which summary sentences best convey the overarching idea of my essay and putting those first, all I need to do is to make small changes to connect the other ideas (and sentences) to one another and to my chosen focus. I've highlighted these changes (by putting them in italics) in the paragraph I have come up with:

Marriage and his relationships with women in general are central concerns in the poetry of William Carlos Williams. *The short poem* "This Is Just To Say" is written as if it were an act of communication, *a brief note*, between the speaker and his spouse. *The poem* uses vocabulary and grammatical choices to emphasize the material reality of the scene it evokes. Set in a kitchen, the locus of women's work in the period in which it was written, it ties the feelings expressed and evoked in the poem to *the nuclear family and to the kind of marital relationship on which this family was based*. The vocabulary choices in the poem depict the scene as being rich with sensory experience and imply that the relationship between the poem's speaker and the person to whom the poem is addressed is also a sensual one. The emotions expressed in the poem are profound. At the same time, the mode of communication and the "Reply" that Williams wrote later in the persona of the spouse suggest remoteness and even isolation or alienation between the "writer" of the note and its "reader."

Wow! I'm pretty impressed, if I do say so myself. This is good stuff, and it's interesting. With a little more work, it will be ready to be my draft introduction. Then I'll just need to unfold the paragraphs and figure out the conclusion and ... but I get ahead of myself. Let's get this paragraph tied up in ribbon, or baked, or built into the best darn brick shed ever made.

Concluding the Introduction

I'm satisfied that this paragraph, as it presently stands, introduces the topic and describes the argument I will undertake in the essay. It suggests the evidence that I will use (focusing on "This Is Just To Say" and including some evidence about the biographical, social, and historical contexts for the poem). The first sentence introduces the broad topic: Williams's poetry and marriage or relationships with women. What this paragraph lacks, other than a little spit and polish that will come later, is a sentence at the end that points to how my argument contributes to our understanding of the meaning or power of Williams's poetry or of how it imitates life. In this concluding sentence, I want to summarize the difference between my findings and what a casual reader might think about the poem (plums! icebox! delicious!). It is perhaps the second most important sentence of your essay (next to your very first one), as it tells your reader about the value of reading your essay. So let's make it the best that we can.

READING AND REREADING

The study of literature means a lot of reading; we know that. But what is sometimes not made clear is that writing essays about literature means rereading *and* rereading *the central text, the notes you've made about it, and any notes you have from other sources. Rereading supports knowledge and understanding, but it also encourages new connections and deeper thinking.*

In order to come up with this sentence, I have to think hard. I'll reread the paragraph, but I'll also go back to my original impressions of the poem to see what sparked my imagination and my aesthetic appreciation in the first place. Reviewing those notes, I find that there are some ideas that I've moved beyond; I'm not feeling so naughty, for instance, as I once did, overhearing part of a written conversation between two people. I've come to see that as part of the access to intimacy and the domestic scene that the poem gives me. But I see that, in general, I was interested in the depiction of the marital relationship, the feelings that the poem evoked, and the language it uses in its short 12 lines to convey these things. If I reread my draft first paragraph *again*, I see that I've been working on developing a finer-grained reading of those features of the poem, and that's what I'd like to communicate in my final sentence. So I want to make sure the sentence refers to feelings, to marriage, and to the language of the poem, and I also want it to refer to the learning I've done in the work I've undertaken since my first reading of the poem.

Let's try out a sentence: *"This Is Just To Say" is a poignant account of the potential for both intimacy and alienation in the nuclear marriage.* Now that's pretty good; I like it. But it says nothing about language. I have lots of specific things to say about language in the body of the essay. But what's the best way I can convey that here? Something about how the poet uses language to convey this potential for intimacy and alienation or about how he conveys it in such a short space on the page, in so few words, might work. So let's add something about that: *"This Is Just To Say," in only 12 short lines and a total of 33 words (including the title), manages to convey a poignant account of the potential for both intimacy and alienation in the nuclear marriage.* How's that? Like it? I'm good with it. Now let's look at the paragraph with that sentence added:

> Marriage and his relationships with women in general are central concerns in the poetry of William Carlos Williams. The short poem "This Is Just To Say" is written as if it were an act of communication, a brief note, between the speaker and his spouse. The poem uses vocabulary and grammatical choices to emphasize the material reality of the scene it evokes. Set in a kitchen, the locus of women's work in the

period in which it was written, it ties the feelings expressed and evoked in the poem to the nuclear family and to the kind of marital relationship on which this family was based. The vocabulary choices in the poem depict the scene as being rich with sensory experience and imply that the relationship between the poem's speaker and the person to whom the poem is addressed is also a sensual one. The emotions expressed in the poem are profound. At the same time, the mode of communication and the "Reply" that Williams wrote later in the persona of the spouse suggest remoteness and even isolation or alienation between the "writer" of the note and its "reader." "This Is Just To Say," in only 12 short lines and a total of 33 words (including the title), manages to convey a poignant account of the potential for both intimacy and alienation in the nuclear marriage.

Looks good. I think it provides an informative and interesting opening for my reader, one that shows them the value of reading the whole essay and also gives them that all-important sense of having learned something already, just by reading the paragraph. It may still change as I work on the rest of the essay. But it's not going to get worse than this, and it provides a strong template to guide me as I write the rest of the essay, in which everything will pertain to one or other of these statements.

A VARIATION: AN ESSAY WITHOUT SECONDARY SOURCES

We wrote our draft introduction in response to an assignment that required us to use a full range of secondary sources, including reference works and critical materials. Often, students are asked to write essays without evidence sources other than the work of literature. This requirement is especially true for exams and midterm tests in which you will often be given a piece of literature to analyze. So let's investigate how to write an essay about literature without using secondary sources. You can use the same method to develop an answer to an essay question on an exam or midterm, so it's a useful method to learn.

Let's start by going back to the first chart I made in Chapter 6, based on evidence gathered only from the poem itself and with the idea of "marriage" exchanged for one of "domesticity"—because the married relationship, while hinted at, is not delineated directly in the text:

First Version of My Chart: Evidence from Poem

	MATERIAL REALITY	DOMESTICITY	SENSUOUSNESS	EMOTION
Poem	"*the* plums" 2 "*the* icebox" 4 "breakfast" 8 "that" 3, "which" 5 (deictics)	Title "I/me," "you" "icebox" 4 "breakfast" 8 (domesticity) "you were probably saving" 6–7	"I have eaten" 1 "delicious" 10 "sweet" 11 "cold" 12	Title "I/me," "you" "Forgive me" 9

From this chart I can write subtopic sentences, as follows:

MATERIAL REALITY: In "This Is Just To Say," William Carlos Williams uses definite articles, concrete nouns, and deictics (pointing words), which emphasize the material reality of the scene evoked by the poem. The poem itself reminds one of an everyday artefact—a brief note between two intimates.

DOMESTICITY: The poem has a domestic setting and outlines a relationship within that setting between two people living together, the one writing the note-like poem and the one for whom it was written.

SENSUOUSNESS: The poem uses vivid, sensual language to describe the plums and to imply a sensual or erotic dimension to the relationship between the poem's speaker and the person to whom the poem is addressed.

EMOTION: The title of the poem and the request to "Forgive me" reinforce the impression that the relationship is emotional as well as material and sensual.

From these sentences, I can prepare a draft introduction and thesis statement for the little essay that I'm writing. I've changed a few words and phrases, and I've also revised the order of the sentences from the list above, so as to go from the broadest observation to more particular ones.

> "This Is Just To Say," by William Carlos Williams, has a domestic setting and outlines a relationship within that setting between two people living together, the speaker of the poem and the person to whom it is addressed. In it, the poet uses definite articles, concrete nouns, and deictics (pointing words), which emphasize the material reality of the scene evoked by the poem. The poem itself is written in the form of a note, from "me" to "you," which suggests a brief, everyday communication between intimates. "This Is Just To Say" uses vivid, sensual language to describe the plums and to imply an erotic dimension to the relationship. The title of the poem and the request to "Forgive me" reinforce the impression that the relationship is emotional as well as material and sensual.

Now I need that summary sentence at the end, the one that says how my reading of the poem contributes to our understanding of the meaning, power, or construction of the poem. Can you think of one? How about something like this: *In a few lines and a handful of words, Williams creates an image of a rich and dynamic relationship and a picture of domestic love that is equally material, sensual, and emotional.* That's fine. So here's our paragraph:

> "This Is Just To Say," by William Carlos Williams, has a domestic setting and outlines a relationship within that setting between two people living together, the speaker of the poem and the person to whom it is addressed. In it, the poet uses definite articles, concrete nouns, and deictics (pointing words), which emphasize the material reality of the scene evoked by the poem. The poem itself is written in the form of a note, from "me" to "you," which suggests a brief, everyday communication between intimates. "This Is Just To Say" uses vivid, sensual language to describe the plums and to imply an

erotic dimension to the relationship. The title of the poem and the request to "Forgive me" reinforce the impression that the relationship is emotional as well as material and sensual. In a few lines and a handful of words, Williams creates an image of a rich and dynamic relationship and a picture of domestic love that is equally material, sensual, and emotional.

That's a perfectly good introduction to a short essay on this poem. We've introduced the topic in the first sentence (the poem and the relationship it represents), we've indicated specific evidence that will support each section of the argument, and we've made a statement about why someone might be interested in reading our essay.

You'll have noticed that the kinds of conclusions about the poem we've come to in each of these sample introductions are quite different. In the first essay, the secondary sources allow us to come to more definite conclusions about the sort of relationship portrayed in the poem and, significantly, to slightly more skeptical conclusions, ones that are more strongly related to the social and historical moment of the poem. The other introduction discusses the poem strictly in the terms that the poem offers within itself. The one essay isn't better than the other, but the thing to notice is that an essay with secondary sources isn't just longer than an essay without them: it's more complex, and it comes to conclusions that are broader and more definitively related to the context within which the work of literature was written and has been read.

TROUBLESHOOTING THE INTRODUCTION AND THESIS STATEMENT

Before leaving your introduction and thesis statement, read it again, carefully (out loud?), and ask yourself the following questions:

- *Does it state your topic?*
- *Does it offer answers to the basic questions we ask about literature?*

- *What does it mean?*
- *How does it work?*
- *Why does it produce the effects it does?*
- *Does it argue inductively, moving from the particular to the general?*
- *Are the statements logically connected?*
- *Is each word in its place, and does each place have a word to go in it?*

CONCLUSION

Your thesis statement is the most important part of your essay. It tells people why they should read your essay and what they will learn if they do. To teach someone something, you have to be knowledgeable, clear, and precise. So base your argument on evidence, make the relationships between your statements logical, and use language that exactly conveys what you want to say. Remember that your mission is to explain some aspect or feature of a beautiful, moving, complex piece of literature. If you work from evidence, reason inductively, and write well, you will share with your reader the "aha!" moment that you had when you first figured out something special about the literature you are studying. That's what it's all about!

REVIEW QUESTIONS

1. Define and give an example of deductive reasoning.
2. Define and give an example of inductive reasoning.
3. What should the last sentence of your introduction contain?
4. Can you complete the following statement in a logical and meaningful fashion: "Since the beginning of time ..."?
5. What should you do if your introduction or thesis statement just isn't working?

CHAPTER EIGHT

Writing the Body of the Essay

AFTER YOU'VE COLLECTED AND ORGANIZED YOUR EVIDENCE and crafted your argument, writing the rest of the essay is easy. The body paragraphs will each make a point contributing to your argument, and each will highlight the evidence that supports that point. The subject for each body paragraph is provided by your subtopic sentences. After you've roughed in these paragraphs, you can revise to make sure that each one is complete and well structured, follows neatly upon the previous one, and provides a transition to the next one. Your conclusion will summarize what you have done and perhaps point to the broader implications of your argument.

THE BODY PARAGRAPHS

The real beauty of basing your essay on carefully collected and arranged evidence will now become apparent, as the body of your essay unfolds from the hard work you've already done. Let's return to the introduction and thesis statement, broken now into sentences that very closely resemble the subtopic sentences that we wrote to summarize each of the sections of our evidence. These sentences will provide our topics for each paragraph. (We'll polish them up for the final draft, so they aren't exactly the same as the sentences in the thesis statement, but, for now, we'll leave them as they are.)

After each sentence, I'll list the evidence from our chart that belongs to it. I've used short forms here to refer to the evidence, but, in your draft, you might want to cut and paste the evidence from your files into place under the topic sentence of the paragraph you're working on. That way, you will see clearly how the essay can take shape when good evidence is combined with careful and imaginative thinking.

Let's start with the first sentence here, and list the bits of evidence after it:

1. Marriage and his relationships with women in general are central concerns in the poetry of William Carlos Williams.
   - *Biography: Williams's marriage* (reference works)
   - *Nuclear family* (social and historical contexts)
   - *Marriage is central concern* and *Williams and women?* (criticism)

I think I will rearrange the evidence a bit so that it flows more logically from the first sentence. I want each sentence to follow upon the previous one, so I want them to be linked by topic or idea. After my rearrangement, the outline for my first paragraph looks like this:

1. Marriage and his relationships with women in general are central concerns in the poetry of William Carlos Williams.
   - *Marriage is central concern* (criticism)
   - *Biography: Williams's marriage* (reference works and criticism)
   - *Williams and women* (criticism)
   - *Nuclear family* (social and historical contexts)

From this outline, and with the full texts of the evidence inserted in the appropriate places, I can write up a paragraph such as the following one:

Marriage and his relationships with women in general are central concerns in the poetry of William Carlos Williams. Critics such as Charles Altieri, Theodora Graham, and Celia Carlson all make note of these preoccupations. According to Graham, "In the drama of their life together, one of the most compelling stories he knew, Williams portrayed himself as the tormented artist, repeatedly tempted to overthrow his conventional life—represented by Flossie—and repeatedly retreating into the familiar and certain still center she provided" (170). Williams and his wife were married for many years ("William Carlos Williams"), although his unfaithfulness was a topic of emotional distress for them both (Graham). The struggle of William Carlos Williams to define and enjoy his marriage is representative of the broader struggle in American society over the nature and structure of marriage (A. Carlson; Brown).

So far, so good. I've been able to draw on my research to support each point, and I've connected each sentence by topic with the previous one. I can do this for each paragraph, integrating the evidence I've collected into sentences that articulate my own argument.

BE GOOD TO YOUR READER

Be kind to your reader and help them get the most out of your essay with the least effort. Making sure each sentence follows on from the one before is one way to help your reader follow your train of thought: abrupt changes in topic are hard to keep track of, and unfinished ideas are difficult to absorb. If each of your paragraphs has a clear relationship to the main argument, the reader feels that they are gathering momentum and accruing value in the course of reading your essay. Errors in grammar, spelling, punctuation, and word choice slow the reader and make them puzzle (unnecessarily) over what you really mean. Remember, you are the teacher in your essay: make your message clear, and make it worth the reader's time and effort.

But I'm still missing something: a concluding sentence for the paragraph. Other than the thesis statement, these concluding sentences are the most important parts of your essay. They serve two functions. The first is that they assert the relevance of these ideas and this evidence to the overall argument. The second is that they provide a transition to the next paragraph. If I remind myself of the topic of the next paragraph and the argument of the essay as a whole, it will be easier to write the concluding sentence for my first body paragraph.

The argument of the essay as a whole, as I know quite well by now, is that "This Is Just To Say" is an extraordinary and intense description of marriage as a relationship between two people—a relationship that has a social and material context and that is conducted, at least in part, through language. I also know that the next paragraph is going to begin with some version of the sentence "The short poem 'This Is Just To Say' is written as if it were an act of communication, a brief note, between the speaker and his spouse." After reviewing these two ideas, I realize I should summarize the first body paragraph by indicating to my reader that I am going to analyze a poem by Williams as a description of marriage crafted in poetry. This sentence will also direct my reader's attention toward the concerns of the next paragraph. I'll try this sentence out as my conclusion: "The description and expression of these struggles in Williams's poetry is, however, a unique record of the personal experience of marriage in twentieth-century America." The draft second paragraph now reads:

Marriage and his relationships with women in general are central concerns in the poetry of William Carlos Williams. Critics such as Charles Altieri, Theodora Graham, and Celia Carlson all make note of these preoccupations. According to Graham, "In the drama of their life together, one of the most compelling stories he knew, Williams portrayed himself as the tormented artist, repeatedly tempted to overthrow his conventional life—represented by Flossie—and repeatedly retreating into the familiar and certain still center she provided" (170). Williams and his wife were married for many years ("William Carlos Williams"), although his unfaithfulness was a topic of emotional distress for them both (Graham). The struggle of William Carlos Williams to define and enjoy his marriage is representative of the broader struggle in American society over the nature and structure of marriage (A. Carlson; Brown). The description and expression of these struggles in Williams's poetry is, however, a unique record of the personal experience of marriage in twentieth-century America.

I'll do this for each of my body paragraphs. Beginning with the topic sentence, I'll put each of the points from my evidence chart in place. I'll draw on the actual evidence to fill in the sentences. I'll move sentences around so that one leads to the next, and I'll devise a concluding sentence that stipulates the relationship of this paragraph to the argument as a whole and that leads to the next paragraph.

FEATURES OF STRONG PARAGRAPHS

Paragraphs are the building blocks of your essay. If you want to build a strong essay, each block must be the right size and proportion, and each must be as solid as the next one: bricks lined up, each one strong and true, mortar firmly in place. A good rule is that paragraphs should not be longer than a page of double-spaced text and not shorter than a quarter of a page. If a paragraph is too long, see if it can be broken into two paragraphs or edited down. If you end up removing a couple of sentences, see if they can be integrated elsewhere, or let them go.

LETTING A GOOD IDEA GO

No one likes to see a good idea or a great sentence end up in the trash. But sometimes we have to let ideas go. It's not a bad thing: in fact, it's a sign that you're a good thinker (more great ideas than can fit in one essay) and that you have a strong sense of your argument (and can tell when something just isn't going to work). Still, it can be painful. Remember this: you had the idea in the first place. It still belongs to you; it will always be part of you. When the right time comes to use it, it will reappear. If it never does, well, it is probably best left resting quietly by itself.

Each paragraph is a mini-essay: each has an opening sentence that states the topic of the paragraph, several (three or four) sentences in the body, and a concluding sentence. If your paragraphs don't follow this format, revise them so that they do. Make sure that the topic of the paragraph is clear and that the evidence presented in the body sentences pertains to the topic and supports the part of the argument you are dealing with in that paragraph. Confirm that you have connected the evidence to the point you are making in the paragraph; remember, you need to elaborate why this particular evidence supports this part of your argument. Check your concluding sentence: does it consolidate the findings of the paragraph and move us forward to the next one?

PARAGRAPH CHECKLIST

- *Does it open with a sentence that conveys the paragraph's topic?*
- *Is it too long or too short?*
- *Are the points in the body of the paragraph supported by evidence?*
- *Have you explained the connections between your evidence and your paragraph's main point?*
- *Does it conclude with a sentence that wraps up the paragraph's findings and moves us forward to the next paragraph?*
- *Is it clear what the relationship of the paragraph is to the argument as a whole?*

WRITING THE CONCLUSION AND REVISING THE INTRODUCTION

The Conclusion

Your conclusion is your chance to remind your readers what you want them to take away with them after reading your essay. It's appropriate to summarize your argument here in much the same way as you did in the introduction. It's a good idea not to use exactly the same words;

vary the sentence structure and vocabulary, and try using some quotations from the poem or the criticism that crystallize your ideas and argument. If you do this, you have concluded the essay *adequately*.

If you are more ambitious, the conclusion is the place to build on the final sentence of your thesis paragraph, in which you've stated the importance of your argument to broader concerns. Let's look at the sentences with which I concluded my two draft introductions in the last chapter. The first is for an essay in which I used secondary sources, and it goes like this:

> "This Is Just To Say," in only 12 short lines and a total of 33 words (including the title), manages to convey a poignant account of the potential for both intimacy and alienation in the nuclear marriage.

The second is for an essay in which I did not use secondary sources, and it goes like this:

> In a few lines and a handful of words, Williams creates an image of a rich and dynamic relationship and a picture of domestic love that is equally material, sensual, and emotional.

In both cases, I note the brevity of the poem, how much it conveys in so few words and lines, and the complex view of an intimate domestic relationship that it provides. If I think hard about what I've learned from writing this essay, I can push these observations a little further. I can say that *Williams shows us that poetry, because of how it uses language and mediates between the personal and the social, is capable of expressing complex, moving, and profound views of the world around us.* I like that, and I think it's a valuable thing for my reader to take away. Note that I haven't proved that poetry *does* do these things, so I don't say that: but I have proved that it *can*, so I say that. Also note that I've stayed on secure ground, supported still by my evidence. I haven't made generalizations about life, about the human condition, about love, and I've stayed right away from "Since the beginning of time" and "It is universally true." But I have made a generalization that is valuable for my reader, one that resonates with the evidence and analysis I have presented in my essay.

TAKING A BREAK

Before you read your draft essay from beginning to end again, take a break. If you can, leave it alone for a day or two or even longer. It's important to "defamiliarize" yourself with what you have written, so you can look at the essay objectively and catch small errors or lapses. When we've been working hard on something, we're often not able to see the difference between what we mean to say and what we have said. It's important for your final version that you are able to see that difference and make small changes to the essay.

Revising the Introduction

After you've taken a break, you can reread the essay from beginning to end and make revisions to your introduction. These revisions will probably not be major. They will strengthen the argument by altering the vocabulary, adding a phrase or two, and perhaps modifying the sentence structure. You might want to add a couple of very brief quotations from the literature, reference works, or criticism, if these are good ways to make your argument clear. These revisions will be based on what you learned as you wrote the body of the essay. Now that you've come full circle, you're just about done!

CONCLUSION

Writing the body of the essay should not be *too* hard if you have lined up evidence in categories, arranged the categories into an argumentative structure, and written a strong thesis statement. It's just a matter of unfolding your thesis statement so that each sentence there begins a paragraph, the substance of which is provided by the evidence you have collected. The analytical reasons that a piece of evidence supports the argumentative contention of the paragraph are implicit in the choice you made to include that evidence in that category. But remember this important advice: your sentences *must* make those reasons explicit. Whenever you feel uncertain, return to two home bases: 1) your research and the evidence it has provided and 2) the thesis statement and the argument it articulates. You're almost done the essay; don't lose heart. If you've got this far and are pleased with the results, the rest will be easy as pie (whatever that means!).

REVIEW QUESTIONS

1. What is the source of your topic sentences for the body paragraphs of your essay?
2. What are the qualities of a strong paragraph?
3. What length is too long or too short for a good paragraph? How can you fix paragraphs that are too long or too short?
4. What does the conclusion of your essay offer your reader?
5. Why should you revise your thesis statement after writing the rest of your essay, and how?

Section Four

POLISH AND
PRESENTATION

CHAPTER NINE

Editing
and Proofreading
Your Essay

YOU ARE READY TO DO THE FINAL EDITING AND PROOFREAD-
ing of your essay. This step is important, and you should always
leave yourself enough time to do it. You may also consider asking
a friend or classmate (one who you think knows the difference
between a comma splice and a sentence fragment!) to proofread
your essay and make suggestions for final changes.

Making sure your essay is letter perfect is important for several
reasons. The first is that you have worked hard on the essay, and you
should respect the results enough to ensure that it goes out wear-
ing its finest clothes, neat and clean and color coordinated (and it's
going to a formal occasion, a wedding or a funeral, not out for coffee
with a friend). The second is that you must do everything you can
to make your reader's experience a positive one, and this means
making sure that there aren't errors that will slow them down. An
incomplete sentence makes your readers wonder where the rest of
the thought went; a misspelling makes them stop and have to figure
out what you were trying to say; the wrong word leaves your readers

scratching their heads, wondering what it is you really mean. The third reason is that you are likely to lose marks for errors in grammar, punctuation, word choice, and spelling. I typically assign 10 per cent of the marks on an essay to these things, and I deduct one mark for each error up to ten. That means that a well-organized essay that uses evidence well and has a good argument can get a worse mark than an essay that doesn't do all those things quite as well if the first essay loses ten marks for mechanical errors and the second doesn't lose any.

BEWARE THE SPELLCHECKER

English is full of homonyms, *which are words that sound the same but mean different things. To/two/too, they're/their/ there, whale/wale/wail—all of these triplets sound identical, but they are spelled differently. And they mean quite different things. Recently, a student wrote the following sentence in an essay for me about* Much Ado About Nothing: *"Claudio rejects Hero viscously, even though they fell in love at first site, because their society is very ridged." Although "viscously" is not exactly a homonym for "viciously," both "site" and "sight" and "ridged" and "rigid" are homonyms, or in the latter case near enough to confuse us. The spellchecker accepted these misspellings, as they are all real words in English. But the spellchecker wasn't right, and the student lost marks for spelling anyway. So proofread carefully, and don't trust your computer with your grades!*

CONVENTIONS OF ESSAY-WRITING STYLE

Diction

Diction means the manner in which something is expressed in words, and it refers to the choice of words, the formality or lack thereof of the sentences, and the degree to which the established rules of grammar are observed. Usually, we want to fit the style of the language to the ideas and purpose of the piece of writing. The essay you have written is a formal argument, and it is logical and rational. The genres that the essay most closely resembles are forensic rhetoric, which tries to prove innocence or guilt in a legal proceeding, and deliberative rhetoric, which tries to show that one social policy is better than another. Both of these genres are also formal, logical, and rational. Their style—accurate and rich vocabulary, powerful and sometimes complex sentences, and an explicit organization of the premises, evidence, and conclusions—suits their subject matter and their audience. The diction you use for an essay should be formal, logical, and rational, and your choices in the essay should suit the ideas you are presenting (which are strong, intelligent, and complex) and the audience for which you are writing (your educated, interested, experienced classmate, whether real or imaginary).

ASPHYXIATED?

When I was a grade-school student, I wrote a short autobiographical piece for my creative writing class about a walk in the woods. In it, I wrote that I was "asphyxiated" by the fragrance of the pine trees. I had a vague sense that the word meant "overcome," generally through the airways, so I thought that it would work. What I was missing was the fact that asphyxiation is usually (no, always) negative in that it causes "asphyxia," which is loss of consciousness perhaps presaging death. "The condition of suspended animation produced by a deficiency of oxygen in the blood; suffocation," according to the OED. *Hmm. Should have looked it up.*

Vocabulary

The vocabulary you use in your essay is a feature of the diction of your essay. If your diction is formal, logical, and rational, your vocabulary should be as well. This means no slang or dialect (words that belong to the modes of communication used by a social or regional subset or particular culture, even if you are part of that culture and it feels like the best and biggest one to you) and no profanity, unless these are words that appear as part of your evidence. But the most important thing about the vocabulary that you choose is that it be *precise*, which the *OED* defines as "[d]istinguished with precision from any other; identified with exactness; particular, exact." Why use precise words? They will best support your argumentative aims. The wider the vocabulary you have at your command, the more precise you can be. Use the dictionary to double-check meanings of words about which you are uncertain. Avoid words that are ambiguous, ones that have more than one possible meaning in the context of the sentence: what works in poetry and song lyrics to express emotion and irony is not going to work in your essay. Mean what you say, and say what you mean.

Connecting Words

Because your essay presents a logical argument that is supported by evidence, you will want to use connecting words that establish the relationship of one statement to another. These include common coordinating conjunctions such as "and," "but," "so," and "or"; subordinating conjunctions such as "because," "although," and "while"; and adverbs more common to formal diction such as "thus," "therefore," "however," "moreover," and "furthermore." You can look these up in the dictionary before you use them, and you should look up any other words like this that you aren't certain how to use. I'll define these ones here and give examples:

FORMAL DICTION

Formal diction doesn't mean using fancy words for the sake of using fancy words. Only use "therefore" instead of "and" if you mean "therefore," that is, if you mean that the second observation you make is a consequence of the first. Remember that you are trying to be as precise as possible, so use the right word, whether it is long or short.

Because these words show the relationships between your ideas and because those relationships are key to how strong and complex your argument is, they are very important. When you are proofreading, try and make sure that your conjunctions and adverbs are as precise and appropriate as you can make them.

COMMON GRAMMATICAL ERRORS

Grammar is the framework and structure of language. It is not just a set of rules any more than the rules of baseball are "just a set of rules." Grammar is what makes our language a language; three strikes and you're out is one of the things that makes baseball baseball and not dodge ball or cricket or polo. Words themselves can't communicate very much. If you know a few words in another language, for instance, but you don't know the grammar, you may be able to get a beer in a bar or find out where the bus station is. But you have been successful not just because you have said "beer" or "bus station" in the language spoken where you are: you've also indicated, by pointing, shrugging your shoulders, or making a face, that *you* (the subject) *want* (the verb) *a beer* (the object of your desire) or that *you* (the subject) *would like* (verb) *to know where the bus station is* (objective phrase). You've expressed grammar with interpersonal gestures and therefore turned a couple of words into acts of communication.

Getting grammar right isn't just a matter of having good manners and evading the wrath of your who/whom-obsessed uncle; it's not the same as which fork to use or how to address your friends' parents or what to wear to a wedding. Grammar is what lets you become part of the occasion in the first place. Imagine that you wrote "If your hamster won't eat its food, feed it to the cat"; you wouldn't be communicating what you want to say to me, unless you wanted me to feed my hamster to my cat. If you wrote in your essay that "Hamlet killed Laertes when he was at his wits' end," I might ask you which of the men you thought was at his wits' end. If you wrote, "The speaker in 'This Is Just To Say' ate the plum from the icebox, which was delicious and sweet," I might wonder why the speaker is eating iceboxes. In each case, you would have used words that I recognize and understand, but you would not have communicated successfully because you did not use grammar correctly. It helps that I understand the words, but, without the correct grammar, I really can't understand what you have to say, and I have to guess. You do not want your reader guessing what you are trying to say: you want your reader awestruck by the brilliance and persuasiveness of your argument.

The three examples above illustrate problems that are quite common in student essays: misplaced modifiers (the hamster and the icebox) and unclear pronoun reference (Hamlet and Laertes and their wits). These mistakes will bedevil your essay, if you make them.

For the curious, here are the three sentences corrected:

- *If your hamster won't eat its food, feed that food to your cat.*
- *When Hamlet was at his wits' end, he killed Laertes.*
- *The speaker in "This Is Just To Say" ate the plum, which was delicious and sweet, from the icebox.*

In my experience, students make other errors much more commonly. The most frequent problems are errors with apostrophes, with demonstrative pronouns, with pronoun agreement, and with verb tense.

Apostrophes

Apostrophes have two functions in our language. The first is to indicate a contraction. Because you are using formal diction, you should never use a contraction in your essay (unless it is part of the evidence you are citing). *Therefore "it's" will never appear in any of your essays, ever, ever, ever.* "It's" is the contracted form of "*it is.*" If you can say "it is," say "it is." The second function that apostrophes have is to indicate possession. These apostrophes will appear in your essay. They will help attach an owner to a thing: "Williams's verse" or "Hamlet's sword" or "Shakespeare's play." Sometimes the ownership is rather abstract, and you have to think about it (for instance, "the play's qualities" or "the verse's rhyme scheme"), but if you remember that the apostrophe hooks things together in a relationship of ownership, then you won't go wrong.

WHERE DOES THE APOSTROPHE GO?

Sometimes, deciding where the apostrophe goes can be tricky. Why? In English, we often indicate a plural form by adding an "s"—so we might have one "dog" or many "dogs" that own something, for example, "breakfast." To figure out whether you want "the dog's breakfast" or "the dogs' breakfast," just switch the bit indicating ownership to a phrase using "of":

> *the breakfast of the dog = the dog's breakfast*
> *the breakfast of the dogs = the dogs' breakfast*

Demonstrative Pronouns

Demonstrative pronouns are "this" and "that" and their plural forms: "these" and "those." They are pronouns because they replace nouns that have previously been mentioned. They are demonstrative because they point to a certain thing—they assume that the object pointed to and the person pointing to it have particular positions in space. We often use "this" in essay writing to refer to something that we have just mentioned: we are pointing back to the thing in the previous sentence. But sometimes we use "this" improperly, to point back with a broad wave of the hand to a set of observations that we wish to refer to. For example, let me repeat my preliminary introduction for the short essay outlined in Chapter Seven, the essay written without secondary sources. Here I've replaced the concluding sentence in order to demonstrate the improper use of demonstrative pronouns:

> "This Is Just To Say," by William Carlos Williams, has a domestic setting and outlines a relationship within that setting between two people living together, the speaker of the poem and the person to whom it is addressed. In it, the poet uses definite articles, concrete nouns, and deictics (pointing words), which emphasize the material reality of the scene evoked by the poem. The poem itself is written in the form of a note, from "me" to "you," which suggests a brief, everyday communication

between intimates. "This Is Just To Say" uses vivid sensual language to describe the plums and to imply an erotic dimension to the relationship. The title of the poem and the request to "Forgive me" reinforce the impression that the relationship is emotional as well as material and sensual. *This* means that the poem is an eloquent, but brief, depiction of domestic love in all its aspects—material, sensual, and emotional.

The last sentence begins with "This," which should refer to a particular previous idea. But the position of the sentence—at the conclusion of the introduction—and the rest of the sentence indicate that I am actually referring to the whole prior argument, as it is described in the paragraph from the beginning to the penultimate sentence. In this context, "this" is not good enough. It struggles to attach to something specific, something concrete. It can't. It's like tethering a hot-air balloon to the ground with a piece of thread; the balloon is too big, too powerful, and it will break the thread and float away. I need to ask myself "This what?" and put the answer in place: "This poem's form, diction, and imagery make it an eloquent, but brief, depiction of domestic love in all its aspects—material, sensual, and emotional."

The bottom line: *use a demonstrative pronoun ("this" especially) only when what it refers to is absolutely crystal clear.* Ideally, use "this," "that," "these," and "those" only to refer to concrete nouns or specific ideas. Better yet, restate that noun or idea after the demonstrative pronoun, adding layers of meaning, if possible: "this sensual and often sibilant language," "these concrete and specific words," "those examples of Williams's radical brevity and simplicity," or "that assertive request for forgiveness." ~~This~~ (whoops!) *These tips* will help you avoid confusing your reader or giving the impression that you are making grand gestures toward vague but undefinable truths, instead of making the exact, brilliant, perceptive, and resonant point you want to make.

Pronoun Agreement

Pronouns must agree with the nouns they replace in *number* and *case*. For example, if you wanted to replace the proper noun "Dave" in the sentence "I gave the ball to Dave," you would use the pronoun "him." Why? Well, you need a *singular* pronoun to get *agreement in number* (Dave is only one guy, so you can't use "them"). And you need to use the *objective case* (Dave is not the subject of the sentence, so you can't use "he"; the word "Dave" is the *indirect object* of the sentence—the one to whom you gave the ball). So you would write "I gave the ball to him." We all know this grammar, and we usually obey this rule when we speak. Sometimes, when we write, we edit a noun (change it from singular to plural, for instance) without changing the pronoun to correspond. Be very careful to align your pronouns with your nouns. By the way, correcting errors in pronoun agreement is one reason among many to let your essay rest for a while before you do the final proofreading; sometimes you will not see the problem even though it's staring you right in the face because you think you've said what you meant to say. Giving yourself a couple of days between finishing the final draft and handing in the essay will help you read what you've actually written, instead of seeing what you think you've written.

Verb Tense

Verb tenses place action relative to the present. Sometimes it can be hard to choose a verb tense to discuss the matter with which essays about literature are concerned. Why would we write about something that happens in a play that is 400 years old in the present tense? Surely it is in the past. But it is a convention of literary criticism to write about events in literature as if the work is present (which it is, in that it is very much alive today) and as if the things that happen in the work happen in the present (which they do, each time we read about them). So we say, "Hamlet kills Polonius." If something happened before the beginning of the play or story, we speak of it in the past tense: "Hamlet once loved Ophelia." If we are talking about two actions or episodes in a work of literature and one happens before the other, we use where we are in our discussion of the work as our "base" present tense and refer to an incident that happened previous to this time using the past tense and to one that will happen after this time using the future tense: "Hamlet is remorseful when he kills Laertes, although he felt no such remorse when he killed the innocent Polonius" or "Hamlet is not remorseful when he kills the innocent Polonius, although he will feel remorse upon killing Laertes."

COMMON ERRORS IN PUNCTUATION AND SENTENCE STRUCTURE

Punctuation and sentence structure are complex systems that shape our communications, and, as with grammar and word choice, they are important to get right in your essay. The most common punctuation and sentence structure problems in the thousand-odd student essays that I've read are errors in the use of the semicolon, comma splices, and sentence fragments.

MAIN (OR INDEPENDENT) AND SUBORDINATE (OR DEPENDENT) CLAUSES

A clause has a subject and a verb that are tied together. Independent clauses can stand alone as sentences, if you want them to. A dependent clause is distinguished by a subordinating conjunction, which introduces this dependent clause as something that qualifies or describes the main part of the sentence (the independent clause). "I go to work" is an independent clause and could stand alone as a sentence. "Because I go to work" is a dependent clause that is supposed to modify an independent clause. "Because I go to work, I get paid" has a dependent clause and an independent clause. Being able to identify dependent and independent clauses is a big help when it comes to proofreading your essay. (And yes, you can start a sentence with "Because"!)

Semicolons

The semicolon is one of the most bold and powerful of all marks of punctuation, and it is an essential tool in writing the kinds of flexible but firm sentences that characterize good essay writing. The key thing to remember about a semicolon is that, unless it is being used in a long list whose items contain commas, *whatever comes after or before it must be a fully independent clause* that could stand alone as a sentence. In other words, each of the word groups that come before and after the semicolon has a subject, a verb, and any objects necessary to complete a sentence. If you could separate—right at the semicolon—the two halves of your sentence and come up with two complete sentences without altering a word, then the semicolon is safe and good. If you can't divide the sentence into two sentences, you need to add to one side or the other whatever is necessary to make the clauses independent. For example, this sentence uses the semicolon correctly: "Hamlet's challenge is to get revenge without compromising himself morally; to do so, he must manipulate his enemies into a situation in which they deserve, morally, to be killed." In contrast, here is a version of the same sentence in which the semicolon is used improperly: "Hamlet's challenge is to get revenge without compromising himself morally; manipulate his enemies into a situation in which they deserve, morally, to be killed." In the second example, the second half lacks a subject so is not an independent clause. When you read over your essay, pay special attention to your semicolons, and make sure they are safe and secure, tucked between two independent clauses.

SEMICOLON OR COMMA? PUNCTUATING LISTS

Semicolons are sometimes used in place of commas in long lists. If the list items have internal commas, we need a stronger punctuation mark to signal the end of an item. The three characters—Laertes, Ophelia, and Hamlet—are the three items of the main list in the following example:

> *Hamlet* also presents us with three youthful characters in crisis: Laertes, who has a driving compulsion to restore meaning to his life through blind, insistent revenge for his father's death; Ophelia, a lonely, frightened, and susceptible creature on the brink of madness; and Hamlet himself, the melancholy,

bitter, and cynical young man who can be reflective and thoughtful, indecisive and hesitant, or rash and impulsive.

In this example, we use semicolons to separate the items in the list, which are each modified by adjectives and adjectival phrases, themselves separated by commas. Generally speaking, if there are commas within the segments you want to itemize in a list, use semicolons to separate the items.

Comma Splices

Unlike the semicolon, the comma is a weakling—or rather it is gentle and sweet and not capable of muscling together two independent clauses. A comma *cannot attach two independent clauses.* The test is the reverse of the one for the semicolon; if both parts of the sentence that are joined by a comma could stand independently as sentences, then you have a comma splice—*and you have made an error.* Here is an example of a comma splice: "Hamlet's challenge is to get revenge without compromising himself morally, to do so, he must manipulate his enemies into a situation in which they deserve, morally, to be killed." Either separate these spliced independent clauses into two sentences (right at the first comma), or replace this comma with a semicolon.

Sometimes you can correct a comma splice by inserting a conjunction to join two independent clauses: "Hamlet is ordered by his father's ghost to kill Claudius, he tries to do so but fails" can be corrected with the addition of the coordinating conjunction "but" and a bit of other massaging: "Hamlet is ordered by his father's ghost to kill Claudius, *but*, when he tries to do so, he fails." In this example we've turned the second clause into a dependent clause that serves as a modifier of the main clause.

Subordinating conjunctions can fix comma splices too. Look at these sentences.

INCORRECT: Hamlet avenges his father's death eventually, this revenge costs him many more deaths.

CORRECT: Although Hamlet avenges his father's death eventually, this revenge costs him many more deaths.

You might think that, if the incorrect sentence about Hamlet's revenge only had the word "however" after its first comma, everything would be okay. Wrong! This is also a comma splice: "Hamlet avenges his father's death eventually, however, this revenge costs him many more deaths." The words "however," "therefore," and "furthermore" (among others) do not have the power to join two independent clauses together; they need a semicolon in front of them if what follows is an independent clause (something that could be a complete sentence on its own).

The important thing to remember is that if you have two independent clauses, a comma *cannot* join them.

THE USE OF THE FIRST PERSON

Many teachers ask students not to use the first person ("I") in their essays. I don't mind if my students do, but you should check with your instructor. What I tell students is to remember that the essay is about what they think, *not what they* believe. *I also tell them that it is implicit that they are the ones speaking in their essays, so they can present their hypotheses and conclusions as statements that emphasize the ideas themselves—readers will understand, unless they are otherwise informed, that the essay writer is the origin of those ideas. But using the first person can be a good rhetorical strategy—for instance, when you want to disagree with a critical commonplace or summarize what you are going to do in the essay. So ask your teacher before assuming that you can't use "I."*

Sentence Fragments

A sentence fragment or incomplete sentence is, as it sounds, a part of a sentence that has been punctuated as if it were a complete sentence. If your sentence lacks any of the essential components of a sentence (a subject that does the action, a verb that says what the action is, and any necessary objects that complete the relationship between the subject and the verb), then it is a fragment. Fragments leave your reader wondering where the rest of the thought got to: they are cliffhangers. When you write fiction or film scripts, you might like to have a cliffhanger of an ending, but, in essays, your readers really like to know what happens.

Fragments tend to be short, and you can usually pick them out of your essay that way. (If you have a "grammar checker" in your word-processing program, it will usually identify fragments for you. It doesn't know how to fix them, however.) But there are certain classes of words that are more likely than others to produce sentence fragments in your work, and we will review two of them here: subordinating conjunctions and conjunctive adverbs.

SUBORDINATING CONJUNCTIONS

Subordinating conjunctions join subordinate or dependent clauses to main or independent clauses. They are very useful to the essay writer because they help connect ideas to each other and interpretations to evidence. One of the most common is "because," which establishes a cause for an effect: "I ate the donuts *because* they were there" or "We know that Hamlet is educated *because*, in Act 1 Scene 2, Claudius prohibits him from returning to school in Wittenberg." Another common subordinating conjunction is "although," which connects an effect with something that is not its cause: "I ate the donuts *although* I was not hungry" or "Hamlet spurns Ophelia *although* he has previously courted her."

In each of the examples I have given, you can identify the main and dependent clauses. The dependent clauses could not stand alone as complete sentences. For this reason, students and other writers are often cautioned not to *start* a sentence with a subordinating conjunction; it's to prevent them from putting forward a subordinate clause as a sentence. But you certainly can start a sentence with a subordinating conjunction: just make sure that the sentence includes an independent clause. For instance, you could say "Although he has previously courted Ophelia, Hamlet spurns her in Act 3 Scene 1" or "Because they were there, I ate the donuts."

By the way, you can also start a sentence with "and" or "but," which are coordinating conjunctions; you just have to make sure you have an independent clause in the sentence: "And, while you are at it, check to see if the comma is in the right place."

COORDINATING CONJUNCTIONS AND SENTENCE FRAGMENTS

Sometimes, we create sentence fragments that begin with coordinating conjunctions (and, but, for, nor, or, so, and yet), conjunctions that, when used correctly, can begin an independent or main clause. In order to be independent, the clause must have a subject, a verb, and any necessary objects, however it begins.

INCORRECT: *I ate the donuts. But was not satisfied.*
INCORRECT: *Hamlet is not a man of violence. But finds himself able to dispatch Rosencrantz and Guildenstern.*

These are fragments because they do not have subjects. To make them independent clauses beginning with coordinating conjunctions, we need to add the implied subjects, the ones named in the original sentences ("I" and "Hamlet" or "he").

CORRECT: *I ate the donuts. But I was not satisfied.*
CORRECT: *Hamlet is not a man of violence. But he finds himself able to dispatch Rosencrantz and Guildenstern.*

Note that the following sentences also use "but" and commas correctly to join together two independent clauses:

CORRECT: *I ate the donuts, but I was not satisfied.*
CORRECT: *Hamlet is not a man of violence, but he finds himself able to dispatch Rosencrantz and Guildenstern.*

You'll have noticed that one kind of sentence with a subordinating conjunction between the two clauses doesn't have a comma in the middle, and the other does. How does that work? When the main clause is first and the subordinate clause is second, you don't need a comma because the end of the main clause and the beginning of the subordinate clause is indicated by the conjunction: when we hear "although," we know a subordinate clause is on its way. When you start the sentence with a subordinating conjunction, you need the comma to indicate where the subordinate clause stops and the main clause begins—the main clause is *that* important.

HOWEVER ...

"However" is the rock on which many sentences in essays founder. It's a very useful word; it introduces a piece of interpretation that is supplementary to the main interpretation, an insight or piece of evidence that serves to complicate and give texture to the main argument. Good use of the word "however" is a marker of exactly the kind of essay you want to write: one that acknowledges and embraces the complexity of the work you are studying and of the interpretation it deserves. However, "however" can cause problems for us all.

Briefly, "however" is actually two different words. One is a conjunctive adverb (see main text), which shows a relationship between two independent clauses, and it is generally treated in the ways I've described under "Conjunctive Adverbs": "There was no good reason for me to eat the donuts; however, I did."

The other way we use "however" is as an adverb of degree. An adverb of degree describes an amount or intensity of whatever is meant by the verb: "I dislike donuts extremely but eat them anyway." Here's an example of "however" as an adverb of degree: "However much I dislike donuts, I can't resist eating them and wish that Professor Randall wouldn't leave a big box in the mailroom every Tuesday morning." However you put it, donuts are a problem.

CONJUNCTIVE ADVERBS

Adverbs typically describe verbs: they are about how things are done. Conjunctive adverbs usually connect two main or independent clauses and show relationship between the actions they represent. They can show cause and effect ("Hamlet fears that Claudius will go to heaven if he is killed at prayer; *consequently*, he is unable to take action in this scene"), contrast ("Ophelia is emotional in the extreme; *in contrast*, Gertrude is repressed, at least until confronted by Hamlet in her closet"), or difference ("Polonius is a buffoon when alive; *however*, his death ironically puts him at the center of the action"), and any number of other relationships between the two clauses.

When two clauses are joined by a conjunctive adverb, the main clause ends with a semicolon. Unlike sentences that include subordinating conjunctions, the order of the clauses connected by conjunctive adverbs cannot be reversed: you can't say "In contrast, Gertrude is repressed, at least until confronted by Hamlet in her closet; Ophelia is emotional in the extreme."

While the clauses can't be reversed, you can start a sentence with a conjunctive adverb. When you do that successfully, the conjunctive adverb links a set of statements made in the preceding sentence or sentences with the substance of the sentence in which it appears. We might say, for instance, "There was no good reason for me to eat the donuts. However, I did." Or, after a long and evidence-rich account, over several paragraphs, of how Hamlet struggles to control his passions with his reason, you might start a paragraph as follows: "Consequently, Hamlet's success leads to his failure to act: his reason has mastered his passion, and without passion he cannot fulfil his father's requests."

OUR BAD HABITS

Once I got an essay back from being peer reviewed by a journal. The reviewers' reports were good, but there was one comment that has stuck with me: "the author has an unholy fondness for semicolons." *The implications were rich and dire: in some way, my relationship with semicolons was obsessive, heretical, probably even erotic, and definitely neurotic. What to do? I've been to semicolon rehabilitation, and I go to regular meetings of semicolons anonymous, but I still have to watch myself and the key that rests so neatly under my right hand's pinkie finger, always tempting me to use it.*

It is likely that you have your own small weaknesses in the realm of punctuation; we all do. I hope that you are not as far gone as I was about semicolons, and, if you are, that you get help. But it is worth your while to look over your essays when you get them back to see if there is a particular error that you make more than others. If so, you can talk to your teacher or a trusted peer, seek counsel at your school's writing center (if there is one), and look for information online. In this chapter, I've tried to cover the errors I see most commonly, but we are all individuals and will each have our own foibles when it comes to writing.

CONCLUSION

Proofreading your essay carefully will pay off. You will prevent yourself from losing marks that you don't need to lose, and you will ensure that your reader can grasp the argument you have to offer fully and readily. When you feel more confident using complex sentence forms and marks of punctuation that you don't use in everyday writing, you can write more powerfully and convey more complex ideas. Proofreading is better done after leaving the essay for a couple of days, as then you can be more certain that you will read what you have written and not what you think you have written. If it helps to read the essay out loud, so as to slow yourself down and make sure you pay attention to every word, then do so. If it helps to have someone else go over the essay and check for errors, then find that someone—you can repay the favor, and you will both get better grades! It's easy to lose steam right at the end of the process: but stick out the last bit of work, and proofread as carefully as you can. And if you feel an "unholy fondness for semicolons" (or any other punctuation mark) coming on, seek help immediately.

REVIEW QUESTIONS

1. What kind of diction should you use in an essay?
2. Why is your spellchecker sometimes wrong?
3. How should you use a semicolon?
4. What is a comma splice?
5. What use can the dictionary be in polishing your essay and producing the final version?

CHAPTER TEN

Documenting Your Sources and Presenting Your Work

YOUR ESSAY IS JUST ABOUT READY TO HAND IN. THE LAST things you need to do are 1) to make sure that you have documented your sources correctly, and 2) to check that you are presenting your essay in a way that either meets your instructor's expectations or is conventional to literary studies. In this chapter, we will review the reasons for documenting sources and following the conventions of presentation. We will also discuss how to handle the inclusion of images in your essay or the presentation of the essay in a multimedia format. I won't bother to give you specific instructions about documentation, as your instructor will tell you which model they want you to follow and direct you to resources to support your work. But some general guidelines can be useful.

REASONS FOR DOCUMENTING SOURCES

In the broadest sense, we document our sources to identify, precisely, how our essays fit with the history of scholarship on the topics with which they are concerned. When I write an essay, I want to show my readers that I have reviewed thoroughly the existing intelligence on the range of topics about which I am writing, including criticism of the literature with which I am dealing, criticism of the author's works in general, assessments of the literary culture of the period, and any other particular areas with which I am concerned, such as gender relations, education, or a certain strain of philosophy. I also want readers to be able to look at my sources if they want to— perhaps they are curious about an area I treat only tangentially, or perhaps they are concerned about the accuracy of my interpretation of the source material. So I need to provide enough information for them to locate the sources I have used. Journals and book publishers normally require that information be presented in a standardized format, which makes it easier for editors and readers to tell if the information is complete and accurate.

For all essay writers, one of the reasons to document sources is that readers will want to see clearly what is original to the author of the essay and what comes from the work of others. For both professional literary critics and students, plagiarism is a very serious charge that can result in severe setbacks and punishments. Plagiarism is the use of another's work, either directly or in close approximation, without acknowledgment. It's a form of theft: intellectual property may be abstract, but it is nonetheless a real form of property in national and international law. Intellectual property is also an important cornerstone of any college or university because these institutions exist primarily to generate ideas and disseminate knowledge. Without intellectual property, we wouldn't have much art, many novels, or much of the technological innovation we enjoy; we would lack these cultural "products" that are so important to our societies, our economies, and our senses of ourselves.

In most universities and colleges, it is incumbent on the student to know what plagiarism is: ignorance and accident are not excuses. In most universities and colleges, there are significant penalties for being found guilty of plagiarism. For your own safety, you should know what plagiarism is and how to prevent it happening in your work.

If you are unable to document your sources without the essay beginning to appear as a network of quotations and ideas from other scholars, then you need to go back to your evidence, read through it again, organize it better, and craft an argument that is supported by, *but not created by*, the sources you have used. I'll repeat: there is no excuse for plagiarism, and there are no accidental ways to commit it.

WHAT'S A PARAPHRASE?

A paraphrase is a rewording of something written or spoken by someone else. You should paraphrase when you want to summarize a much longer argument from your source. You should not just change the order of words, or replace a few of them, and call the result a paraphrase. You need to recast the idea in your own mind, using your own words. When you could use a quotation of reasonable length instead of a paraphrase, do so. A quotation makes it clear to your reader what is your work and what is not. Students are sometimes tempted to insert paraphrases between quotations from the same source, so it doesn't look as if their essays are entirely composed of the work of others. If that's a problem you are having, paraphrasing is not the solution. You have to go back to your evidence and start the process of composing your own argument rather than reproducing the arguments presented by your sources.

PLAGIARISM AND PRIDE

The single most powerful antidote to plagiarism is pride in your own work. If you have worked hard, gathered evidence carefully, organized it well, and constructed an argument that is compelling, precise, and well supported, then you should be glad to take ownership of your essay. Ensuring that you document your sources is one way to show your pride in your work and to distinguish this work as your own.

Documentation Practices

There are several different systems of documentation used in the humanities. In English studies in North America, the most common is the Modern Language Association (MLA) system, which is codified in the *MLA Handbook for Writers of Research Papers*, now in its eighth edition (2016). Some journals also use a system based on *The Chicago Manual of Style*, but most instructors will ask you to use the MLA system.

BIBLIOGRAPHY OR LIST OF "WORKS CITED"?

What is the difference? A bibliography includes all of the works that you have consulted in preparing your essay. It may contain works that you have read (in whole or in part) but that you have not quoted or paraphrased or otherwise directly referred to in the essay. A list of works cited is just that—a list of the works that you have quoted, paraphrased, or directly referred to or named in your essay. Check with your instructor for advice about which to prepare for your essay.

Within each of these systems, there are various options. You should check whether your instructor wants you to use footnotes or endnotes or parenthetical citations (in which you put the author's name and the page number of your source in parentheses after the quotation or paraphrase, and this "parenthetical" material refers readers to a list of "Works Cited" for complete information about your source). Some instructors are very firm about their preferences in these matters. Others (me, for instance) simply ask that students ensure that all quotations and paraphrases are attributed and that all works cited are documented thoroughly and consistently.

There are online resources to help you with your documentation, but the best source is a printed version. There will be copies of popular handbooks in your library, and there are style and grammar guides that reproduce the basics of each system of documentation along with helpful information about comma splices and the virtues and vices of the semicolon. Consult your instructor for more guidance on what resources to use to guide your documentation practices.

PRESENTING YOUR WORK

Layout and Order

At its most basic, your essay's format should allow for easy reading and leave room for comments by your instructor on every page. Unless your instructor gives you specific instructions otherwise, you will be safe if you do the following:

- use a 12-point font and double space;
- format your document with margins of at least 1 inch (2.5 cm) on all sides;
- number your pages;
- put your "Bibliography" or "Works Cited" on a separate page at the end;
- make sure your name, your instructor or teaching assistant's name, your student ID number, and the course number and section are displayed at the top of the first page (you don't normally need a cover page, and this information can go at the top left corner of the first page);
- staple or fasten the whole together with a paper clip, unless you are delivering it electronically. (Don't send paper clips through the Internet! I'm kidding.)

TITLES

Titles of books and book-length works, such as long poems, should be underlined or italicized. Titles of poems and short stories should be placed in quotation marks, without any underlining or italicization. If you are unsure whether the title of a long poem or a short play should be italicized or enclosed in quotation marks, ask your instructor or, in a pinch, follow the practice of a reputable critical source or the advice given in the MLA Handbook.

Some teachers will give you additional guidelines or rules they would like you to follow. I prefer not to have the justification on both sides of the page, for example, as I find it harder to read. But, as I receive my students' essays electronically, it's not hard for me to adjust this feature myself. If your teacher gives you guidelines, follow them; if not, the list above is sufficient.

Illustrations

You may want to include illustrations in your essay. Doing so is easy with modern word-processing and image-manipulation computer programs. There are two important things to remember.

First, an image that looks good on the Internet will not necessarily look good on the printed page. Our computer screens are relatively low resolution: they display only about 72 pixels per inch. Printers print a lot more dots per inch than computer screens display. If the image you have chosen is not printing clearly, this difference is probably the reason. For your purposes, you want an image that is at least 150 dots or pixels per inch. You can usually resize the image with image-manipulating software.

ELECTRONIC FILE FORMATS

There are lots of different forms in which to save electronic files. Some of these are universally readable, and some are not. As a rule, text files saved in "rich text format" can be read by all computers and edited by the reader. "PDF" files can also be read by all computers, but most teachers like to write in the files, and most won't have the software necessary to edit a PDF. If you are creating a multimedia essay, ask your instructor what form to deliver the file in. Getting it right the first time will save everyone time and anxiety.

Second, images on the Internet usually belong to someone. You can usually use an image from the Internet for educational purposes (and not for formal publication or distribution) if you give credit to the originator. It is sometimes hard to track down the source for an image on the Internet, however, as digital media is readily copied from site to site. Do the best you can to find out as much as you can about the image: if it is a painting, for example, see if you can find out the artist, the date, and the present location of the work. Include the information you have about the work in a caption, and include the information about where you got the image in your list of works cited. In the handbook that you use or on the Internet itself, there should be information about how to document an image in your list of works cited; otherwise, you can ask your teacher.

MULTIMEDIA AND THE LITERARY ESSAY

I have had students submit essays produced using slideware programs or as web pages or websites. When essays are presented in these forms, they use visual composition to help construct the argument and visual images as evidence in support of the argument. Multimedia essay writing can be really enjoyable, as it allows you to use your creative capacities in ways not normally encouraged by the essay form. Still, it's not just a matter of adding some sparkle and glitz. There are effective ways of using multimedia tools in the literary essay, and it's important that you think through what will work to support your success.

SLIDEWARE

Slideware, which you probably know by the brand name of its most popular form, is as ubiquitous in academia as it is in business and government. It's easy to use badly but not hard to use well. The key is to use it thoughtfully and to avoid the ready-made templates that, according to Edward Tufte, "weaken verbal and spatial reasoning and almost always corrupt statistical analysis" (Tufte 3). For more about the perils of PowerPoint, see Tufte's The Cognitive Style of PowerPoint™: Pitching Out Corrupts Within.

If you are presenting your essay using multimedia tools, you should be conscious of using principles and components of design to craft your work. There are many good tutorials on visual composition on the Internet and many good basic books in the library and in bookstores. I won't review those here for you; if you are given the option of submitting a multimedia essay, your teacher will go over basic use of composition, color, form, space, pattern, proportion, and contrast in order to create a pleasing product. They will also help you work with the technology that you are using to make the best use of your ideas and take advantage of the particular media you are working with: desktop publishing, slideware, and hypertext mark-up language (HTML, the basic code of web pages) all have strengths and weaknesses, and you should be aware of them as you work your way through your project.

Basic design knowledge is not enough, however, to "write" effectively in multimedia form. Even a glance through a typical magazine spread will show you how carefully illustrations and composition are integrated with the text and how they contribute to the power and meaning of the words on the page. Visual communication is different from verbal communication, and the combination of the two is different still. Consistent use of composition, color, and illustration placement can contribute to the structure of your multimedia essay: in effect, you can use design elements to construct a visual grammar, so your design can contribute to how your essay gets its message across and to how much pleasure, knowledge, and satisfaction you can give your reader—or should we say viewer?

In addition to compositional features, multimedia allows you to add illustrations, as we've discussed above. Illustrations in a multimedia essay should not be used simply as decoration. Illustrations in essays must have some relationship to the text to which they correspond. Basically, we can divide these relationships into three types: exemplary, complementary, and supplementary.

Exemplary Illustrations

Exemplary illustrations give examples of things that you are writing about in the essay. For example, for our essay on William Carlos Williams's poem "This Is Just To Say," we might want to add a picture of an icebox as an illustration. The effect on the reader would be to make concrete and visual the idea of the icebox in the poem, which might support two aspects of our argument: one, the materiality of the scene, and two, the era in which the poem is set.

The problem with exemplary illustrations lies in the fact that visual images are specific and exclusive: that is, the icebox in the picture is a certain kind of icebox, and the time it represents is a specific time. It's easier to see this point with a different example: if I write the word "dog," that might conjure an image of a certain sort of dog in your mind, but possibly not. And even if it did, you would know that other readers might well think of a different sort of dog or about several sorts. But a picture is a picture of *a* dog (a small or a big dog, a border collie or a mutt, a fierce or gentle-looking dog, and so on). It does not suggest "dog" in general. So you should realize that, when you use exemplary illustrations, you might well be limiting the imagination and thinking of your reader more than is useful for your argument. For the purposes of your argument, for example, it doesn't matter if the icebox is small or large, painted or not. But the picture will specify those characteristics, and it will shape your reader's understanding of your point.

Complementary Illustrations

Complementary illustrations echo the verbal statement or statements they accompany. For example, if you analyzed a scene from *Hamlet* in an essay, you might illustrate that section of your essay with a picture of the scene. You might especially want to choose a picture that emphasizes aspects that you are discussing in the verbal part of the essay. Complementary illustrations can reinforce your point and offer your reader more evidence to support your argument.

The danger of using complementary illustrations is twofold. First, they can contradict your verbal analysis—for example, they might show a choice by an actor or a director for Hamlet's behavior that is not consistent with how you understand the play or the scene in question. Second, they might serve to be more exemplary than complementary: an image of a production of *Hamlet* is an image of a specific production that happened in a particular place, at one time, and featured certain actors. If the specificity of the image is such that it encourages the reader to consider concrete issues of staging or of fashions in props and costumes, then you might have undermined the degree to which the illustration can enhance your argument (unless, of course, your essay concerns the staging, props, or costumes used in a particular period or production).

Supplementary Illustrations

Supplementary illustrations extend the argument outside the boundaries within which the verbal argument is made. Let's say you were analyzing a landscape poem and were focused on the ways in which the poet creates the illusion of infinite space before the viewer. In searching for illustrations, you are inspired: an artist's painting of what they believe outer space to look like has many features in common with the poem you have analyzed. You choose to illustrate the part of your argument that concerns the illusion of infinite space with this painting of outer space.

If you are successful, your reader will see a correspondence between the two and will understand the relevance of your argument to arguments beyond the question of how we imagine landscape and connect your argument, with the help of the illustration, to questions of how we imagine knowing what is unknown and conceptualizing that which is infinite and unbounded. If you are unsuccessful (that is, if you haven't clearly articulated the argument or if you haven't hinted at the broader questions to which your argument might apply), then your reader might wonder what the connection is between the text and the illustration—and be distracted by the wondering.

When you compose a multimedia essay, you need to take care to use the components and principles of design to support the structure and sequence of your essay and its argument. When you choose illustrations for a multimedia essay, you should assess what you are doing with the illustration in terms of the argument: Are you offering an example? Are you reflecting the argument? Or are you extending it to realms outside those with which you deal directly in the essay? Assessing the function of your design and of your image choices will help you use multimedia tools to make an even more effective argument than you otherwise could.

LAST-MINUTE CHECKS

Before handing in your essay, you should do one final reading of it. In particular, you should check the following:

- Is the word or page count close to what the assignment called for?
- Have you spelled the instructor's name correctly and included the name of the teaching assistant, if there is one?
- Is everything absolutely perfect in the first paragraph? Is the first sentence the best sentence you have ever written?
- Have you numbered your pages?
- Have you attached the "Works Cited" or "Bibliography"?
- If you're happy with the essay and you have answered "yes" to all these questions, then it's time to hand it in.

TALKING TO YOUR INSTRUCTOR ABOUT YOUR GRADE

Sometimes, you will be mystified by your grade. If you are mystified as to why it is so high, you are unlikely to be inspired to approach your instructor, although finding out exactly what you did right can be very useful. But if you are disappointed in your grade and don't understand why it is as low as it is, you should definitely talk to your teacher. Approach them after class or during their office hours to make an appointment, or send a note by email. Remember that your relationship with your instructor is professional: address them by title ("doctor" or "professor," usually), and sign your full name to any written communication (attaching your student number is often helpful too). Make an appointment to see them, and ask for help understanding where you lost marks. It's part of our job to grade, and it's also part of our job to talk to students about their grades. So don't be shy. But don't be defensive either; it's part of your job to learn at university, so you shouldn't expect to have all the answers already. Remember, your professor will need time to recall the details of your paper, so be courteous and allow for this preparation by making an appointment.

CONCLUSION

Documenting the sources of your work is an essential obligation in an essay. It's absolutely vital that you distinguish between what is original to your thinking and what belongs to someone else. Take pride in your work, and document your sources thoroughly and carefully. In addition to helping you produce a better essay, documenting sources supports the mission of the university, which is built on the idea that people's thoughts and scholarly contributions are valuable and important and should be recognized as such. By recognizing the contributions of others, you imply that we should have respect for your work and give you the credit it deserves. You also imply that you are ready to take on the responsibilities that come with being part of the university community, along with the many privileges it offers.

Present your essay in the best possible light by following the guidelines given to you by your instructor or the conventions outlined here. If you include illustrations, make sure to report their sources, and use versions that will print well. If you work in multimedia, take care to be conscious of the ways in which your visual choices affect your argument: they can make it stronger, more vibrant, and more compelling, but they can also undermine it.

Produce your essay as a professional. Spell people's names correctly, and identify yourself fully. Show your pride in your work in every choice you make about its presentation. And have confidence in approaching your instructor if you do not understand why you received the grade that you have. Grading essays is objective, and your teacher has measured particular things in your essay, but they might be able to explain them better. And, of course, your teacher is human and may well have made a mistake that they would like to correct. If you are courteous and composed, you will likely have a good conversation that will strengthen your understanding of the essay form and enhance your essay-writing performance next time. So don't be afraid to approach your instructor; if you do so with respect and maturity, you are bound to get good results.

REVIEW QUESTIONS

1. What is plagiarism?
2. When should you use paraphrases, and when should you use quotations?
3. Can you list some of the features of the conventional presentation of an essay?
4. When do you use quotation marks and when do you use italics to indicate a title?
5. What are the three main relationships between text and image in a multimedia essay?

Section Five

CONCLUSION
AND
REVIEW

CHAPTER ELEVEN

The Process of Essay Writing —A Summary

THE ESSAY-WRITING PROCESS THAT I HAVE DESCRIBED IN THE previous ten chapters is based on evidence and designed to help you craft a compelling and clear argument about how a work of literature instructs, delights, and imitates life. Here is a summary of the process. You can use it to review what you have learned in the book and to check that you have followed all the necessary steps.

COLLECTING EVIDENCE (CHAPTERS 2-5)

At a minimum, your evidence will come from

- your first impressions, and
- your close reading of the text you are writing about.

In addition, you may collect evidence from the following sources:

- other works by the same author or by authors associated with the one on whom you are focusing;
- reference works such as scholarly editions, biographies, dictionaries, and encyclopedias;
- works about the social and historical contexts for the literature you are studying; and
- critical essays and books.

All of your evidence should be

- carefully transcribed, preferably rekeyed rather than cut and pasted into a text file;
- precisely documented; and
- labeled with terms that remind you of the significance you feel the evidence has.

CATEGORIZING EVIDENCE (CHAPTER 6)

Once you have completed your research, you should

- reread all your evidence,
- review the labels you have assigned to it,
- arrange the evidence in categories,
- reduce the number of categories (usually to three, four, or five, depending on the length and complexity of your essay), and
- compose your evidence in a chart that organizes the evidence by category and by source.

Each category should have several pieces of evidence in it, but it is not necessary to have evidence from all sources in each category.

WRITING YOUR THESIS STATEMENT (CHAPTER 7)

To compose your thesis statement,

- read the evidence in each of your categories,
- compose a sentence that reflects the evidence for each category,
- arrange these sentences so that they are linked logically,
- compose an opening sentence that introduces the topic and that is related to all of the categories, and
- compose a concluding sentence that sums up the argument and points to the relevance of your argument to broader questions than the ones you will address directly in your essay.

TROUBLESHOOTING THE THESIS STATEMENT (CHAPTER 7)

Before leaving your introduction and thesis statement, read it again carefully, and ask yourself the following questions:

- Does it state your topic?
- Does it offer answers to the basic questions we ask about literature?
  - What does it mean?
  - How does it work?
  - Why does it produce the effects it does?
- Does it argue inductively, moving from the particular to the general?
- Are the statements logically connected?
- Is each word in its place, and does each place have a word to go in it?

WRITING THE BODY PARAGRAPHS (CHAPTER 8)

Each of your body paragraphs should begin with a variation of the corresponding sentence in your thesis statement. In each paragraph, you should detail that section of the argument, using the evidence from that category to support your claims.

After writing the body of the essay, review your paragraphs and ensure that each

- opens with a sentence that conveys the paragraph's topic,
- is not too long (a page or more) or too short (a quarter of a page or less),
- includes evidence to support each point,
- concludes with a sentence that wraps up the paragraph's findings and moves us forward to the next paragraph, and
- has a clear relationship to the argument as a whole.

CONCLUDING YOUR ESSAY (CHAPTER 8)

Your conclusion

- should remind readers of what you want them to take away with them upon reading your essay,
- should summarize your argument, and
- can develop the ideas in the final sentence of your thesis paragraph in which you've stated the relevance of your argument to broader concerns we have.

PROOFREADING (CHAPTER 9)

Proofread your essay carefully (or share with a classmate, and proofread each other's essays). Check especially for the following common errors:

- homonyms mixed up,
- improperly used connecting words,
- vague or ambiguous use of demonstrative pronouns,

- improperly used apostrophes,
- problems with pronoun agreement,
- problems with verb tense,
- semicolon errors,
- comma splices, and
- sentence fragments, especially those caused by improper use and punctuation of subordinating conjunctions and conjunctive adverbs.

DOCUMENTATION AND PRESENTATION (CHAPTER 10)

It is essential that you document your sources:

- include all necessary information about the source;
- quote rather than paraphrase, where possible;
- include sources and information about any pictures that you use; and
- record all your sources in either the "Works Cited" or the "Bibliography" of your essay.

Present your work according to the instructions you receive about

- page or word count,
- "Works Cited" or "Bibliography,"
- documentation style, and
- margins and font size.

If you do not receive instructions otherwise, follow these guidelines:

- use 12-point font and at least 1-inch margins;
- put your name, your student ID, your instructor's name (correctly spelled), and the course number on the first page, along with your TA's name if relevant;
- number your pages; and
- attach a list of "Works Cited."

CONCLUSION

I said at the beginning of this book that any literate, hard-working student can write an essay that earns an A-level grade. I hope that you can use the advice and processes described in this book to do just that. If you already write A-level essays, then you will have learned more about how you do that, so you will be able to work confidently with more advanced kinds of evidence and in the production of longer and more complex forms of the essay.

What I most hope is that the work you will do in following the guidelines in this book will bring you those thrilling moments of insight and flashes of truth and beauty that are the reward of hard work on the foundations of good essays. Since the beginning of time ... NO, that is not allowed! But let me offer a generalization about literature here. Literature is connected to the best things about us humans—our abilities to read and write and communicate, our emotional intensity, our complex psychologies, and our phenomenal capacities to remember, reflect, regret, and hope. Improving our individual and collective abilities to understand literature and how it affects us and to communicate with each other about those things is a good way to use and share the gifts we have been given. Happy writing. I'll be thinking of you.

Using
Reference Works
(Ch. 3)

ASSIGNMENT: Write a three- to five-page essay (750-1250 words) about "This Is Just To Say" by William Carlos Williams, using the poem and any or all of the following reference works: a dictionary (especially the *OED*), an encyclopedia, a biography of Williams, and a scholarly edition (annotations and introduction). You may wish to review your notes from class and from your close reading of the poem, and look over your responses to the "Guiding Questions" listed on p. 22 of *Writing Essays About Literature*.

To compose this essay, I start by rereading the poem and reviewing my notes, my answers to the guiding questions (p. 22), and the conclusions I came to (see pp. 33). The conclusion I would like to explore further is that the poem is about relationships between people and how these relationships are shaped by the use of language; I want to find out more about how that happens in the poem. I planned to use the *OED*, an encyclopedia (likely *Wikipedia*), and a scholarly edition of the poem to do my research. I also used a biography, in part because Internet searching suggested to me that there was something useful I might want to know about WCW's marriage.

You'll see when you read the sample essay I've composed that I rely on grammatical features as evidence of how the poem works. I know that you might not know what a demonstrative pronoun is, or what the present perfect verb tense looks like. But you are able to ask your instructor (who is something of an expert in these questions), look up words in the dictionary, and even search on the Internet. I asked the Internet, for instance, "I have eaten what verb tense" and it responded, "present perfect." How does it know so much!?

SEARCHING THE INTERNET FOR IDEAS

The Internet is full of great information about everything. You can use the Internet to get ideas and make connections. Internet search results themselves aren't usually credible sources to use in your essay, but they may lead to good sources. For this essay, for instance, I searched for "William Carlos Williams infidelity" which led me to the biography, which is a credible source.

For this kind of essay (a typical essay assigned in literature and writing classes at every level of secondary and postsecondary education), I hope to have an opening paragraph that states the topic and outlines the argument of the essay, three or four body paragraphs, and a conclusion. Each body paragraph should have a topic, and there should be four or five key points made in each paragraph that are a) supported by evidence and b) about that topic. If I gather and arrange my evidence well, then all I have to do is write it up as the story of that evidence. The conclusion at the least will sum up the argument, and at the most point toward further implications or further pathways for research.

****

Katherine Acheson (SN 084310962)
January 20, 2020

The Language of Intimacy in
W. C. Williams's "This Is Just To Say"

Even though it is only 28 words long, "This Is Just To Say" by William Carlos Williams vividly conveys the nature of the relationship between the speaker or writer of the poem and its listener or reader. That relationship is everyday and down-to-earth; it is between people who have a history together; it is sensual and intimate. These qualities are conveyed through the choices the poet makes of words and grammatical features. The vocabulary reinforces the impression of the sensory, material, and experiential world. The use of the definite article ("the"), demonstrative pronouns ("This"), relative pronouns ("that" and "which"), and personal pronouns ("I" and "you") imply a concrete reality which is shared by, and private to, the writer and the reader. The range of verb tenses suggests a shared history, a common present, and the likelihood of a future together. Finally, the request for forgiveness in the final stanza is a mark of complex interpersonal and emotional relations. "This Is Just To Say" makes clear that poetry's value is not restricted to its intellectual or aesthetic powers—it can also represent some of the many ways in which language shapes and reshapes the relationships we have with others in our worlds.

The choice of words in the poem conveys a sense of a material, everyday reality. The nouns ("plums," "icebox," and "breakfast,"

for example) are all concrete things, rather than abstract concepts.
The poem also uses small functional words that are not nouns
to build the perception we have of an actual space in which real
people interact. "The" is a definite article ("the, A.I."), meaning
that it points to an individual or particular thing, rather than to
the concept or generic form of the thing. "The plums" (l. 2) are
specific, physical plums, not metaphors or ideas, and they were
in "the icebox" (l. 4), which is also an object with functional
properties for the people who own it. The poem uses relative
pronouns ("that" and "which") which point to specific things
and distinguish them from other examples of their kind, or from
abstract conceptions of the thing ("that, A.I.a.1" and "which,
I.4.III.7"). "This" in the title is a demonstrative pronoun; it points
from the speaker to the poem itself, at least in its own fiction as a
note between two people ("this, I.1.a"). Finally, "I" and "you" are
pronouns whose meaning is relative to who is doing the speaking.
As readers of the poem, we infer that "I" and "you" know who
each other are and that there is no ambiguity for them in the
communication: the conversation is private to the two of them.
These words, the meanings of which we usually take for granted
and which we often overlook when we think about the vocabulary
of a piece of literature, contribute to the way in which the poem
evokes an actual space in which people go about their daily lives
and the relationships they have in that space.

The vocabulary of the poem also suggests that sensual
and possibly sexual pleasures are routinely shared between the

two people. "Plums" are sweet, rich, and velvety; they are also red or purple, both colors associated with the human body and especially with intimate or inner parts ("plum II.7"). The plums are "delicious," "so sweet," and "so cold"; the experience of eating them is a sensual pleasure. If the language suggests sensuality, the fact that the speaker enjoyed the plums by themself suggests that they denied those pleasures to the reader or listener— pleasures the reader or listener seems to have planned on, as they were "probably/saving [the plums]/for breakfast" (ll. 6-8). The speaker's demand, "Forgive me" (l. 9), can be seen in this context as a slightly dramatic overstatement of transgression and remorse, designed both to acknowledge the sin and to deflect or minimize its punishment. The sexual nuances of the description of eating the plums suggests both physical and emotional intimacy between the speaker or writer and the hearer or reader.

The intimacy of "I" to "you" is reinforced by the use of verbs in the poem. The use of the present perfect tense, "I have eaten," which usually describes an action recently completed, initiates a timeline for the poem's events. Within the timeline, we recognize the time immediately before the speaker ate the plums, when the decision was made, and the time immediately after, when they are experienced as "delicious," "so sweet/and so cold" (ll. 10-12). But there is also the future that didn't happen, signaled by the use of the conditional "were probably/saving" (ll. 6-7) in which the recipient of the poem's wishes were fulfilled, and the future that will happen, in which the recipient does—or does not—accede to the demand to "Forgive me" (l. 9). The verbs describe people who live together and have shared history in which their actions impact each other, and their preferences and potential reactions are known to each other.

When it was published in Williams's *Collected Poems*, "This Is Just To Say" was annotated with a footnote in which readers found another poem, called "Reply." While both poems are by Williams, "Reply" is written in the voice of the recipient of "This Is Just to Say" and is signed "Love. Floss," the familiar name of Williams's wife Florence ("William Carlos Williams"):

"Reply"
(crumped on her desk)

Dear Bill: I've made a
couple of sandwiches for you.
In the ice-box you'll find
blue-berries—a cup of grapefruit
a glass of cold coffee.

On the stove is the tea-pot
with enough tea leaves
for you to make tea if you
prefer—Just light the gas—
boil the water and put it in the tea

Plenty of bread in the bread-box

and butter and eggs—

I didn't know just what to

make for you. Several people

called up about office hours—

See you later. Love. Floss.

Please switch off the telephone.

Like "This Is Just To Say," "Reply" refers to the prosaic, everyday life of a married couple whose long story is made of many short sentences. But unlike "This Is Just To Say," "Reply" is entirely about the material world and the basic needs of the humans within it. The relationship it describes is longstanding and good-humored, even faithful and loving, but it is neither sensual nor sexual. Most importantly, "Reply" implicitly refuses forgiveness by rejecting the dimension of the marital relationship in which sin or betrayal can happen. According to his biographer, Herbert Liebowitz, Williams was routinely unfaithful to his wife, whom he often regarded with contempt and even derision (Liebowitz, Ch. 5). With the additional context provided by the juxtaposition of the two poems in the *Collected Poems*, we can see that the sensual austerity of "Reply" and the request for forgiveness in "This Is Just To Say" together suggest a stand-off, an unresolved tension within the marriage of the two speakers/writers. Between the two poems, then, an unresolved marital drama unfolds. Williams's mastery of the fundamental powers of language to describe the shape and substance of human relationships turns these short poems into rich and nuanced stories about decades of married life.

Works Cited (MLA 8 format)

Liebowitz, Herbert. *Something Urgent I Have to Say You': The Life and Works of William Carlos Williams.* Farrar, Straus and Giroux, 2011.

"plum, n. and adj.2." *OED Online*, Oxford UP, December 2019, www.oed.com/view/Entry/146028. Accessed 6 January 2020.

"that, pron.1, adj., and adv." *OED Online*, Oxford UP, December 2019, www.oed.com/view/Entry/200177. Accessed 6 January 2020.

"the, adj., pron.2, and n.1." *OED Online*, Oxford UP, December 2019, www.oed.com/view/Entry/200211. Accessed 6 January 2020.

"this, pron. and adj." *OED Online*, Oxford UP, December 2019, www.oed.com/view/Entry/200894. Accessed 6 January 2020.

"which, pron. and adj." *OED Online*, Oxford UP, December 2019, www.oed.com/view/Entry/228284. Accessed 6 January 2020.

"William Carlos Williams." *Wikipedia: The Free Encyclopedia*, https://en.wikipedia.org/wiki/William_Carlos_Williams. Accessed 10 January 2020.

Williams, William Carlos. "Reply." *The Collected Poems of William Carlos Williams. Volume I: 1909–1939*, edited by A. Walton Litz and Christopher MacGowan, New Directions Press, 1986, p. 536.

——. "This Is Just To Say." *The Collected Poems of William Carlos Williams. Volume I: 1909–1939*, edited by A. Walton Litz and Christopher MacGowan, New Directions Press, 1986, p. 372.

Bringing in Social and Historical Contexts (Ch. 4)

ASSIGNMENT: Write a four- to six-page essay (1000-1500 words) about "This Is Just To Say" by William Carlos Williams, using the poem and any or all of the following reference works: a dictionary (especially the *OED*), an encyclopedia, a biography of Williams, and a scholarly edition (annotations and introduction). In addition, you must use some sources (reference works and scholarly articles) that provide information about the social and historical contexts for the poem. The aim of the essay is to help us understand the poem in relation to those contexts.

This kind of essay builds on the work you would do for the shorter essay that uses your close reading and reference works to support the argument. To compose this essay, I began by reviewing the poem, my close reading, and the material from reference works that I used in Essay One. In addition, I used databases in my library to look for books, essays, and articles that might help me understand something about how a poem like "This Is Just To Say" comes from and speaks to its social and historical contexts. The poem was published in 1934, so that date provides an anchor for our understanding of the contexts of both its composition and its reception.

THE RESEARCH QUESTION

When we want to talk about the spine of an essay in English studies, we mean the thesis. The thesis is the main statement we are trying to prove in the essay. In other disciplines, especially sciences and social sciences, the process of composing an essay or report hinges on defining the research question. The research question asks, what is the relationship between one thing or phenomenon and another? It might say, "What are the effects of airborne particulates on migratory bird navigation?" or "Do people who exercise daily report higher levels of satisfaction in romantic relationships?" or "Does increasing access to public transit decrease the amount that people drive personal vehicles in urban settings?" It may help you to conceptualize your thesis statement to know that it's just a variation on the research question: it's a question turned into a statement.

For Essay One, my thesis was that the poem shows us one way in which language builds intimacy, as opposed to just reflecting it. I could write this as a question that follows the form of a scientific research question instead: "Does language create intimacy in 'This Is Just To Say'"? It's really just a convention: humanities research typically presents a statement to be argued, while scientific research typically asks a question to be answered. If thinking of your thesis as a research question helps you—especially in the sense that it encourages you to go to your "lab" (your library!) and do some "experiments" (putting ideas from reading together) so as to discover or prove something (Eureka!)—then go for it!

On pages 63–67 I describe my research strategy and process and review some of the things I found out about domestic life for white, middle-class America in the first half of the twentieth century. Labor-saving devices made housework and food preparation easier, but they also spurred changes. Extended families became less common, and the nuclear family (Mum and Dad and kids) became the norm. Middle-class families were less likely to hire domestic help, and working-class families were less likely to be employed as cooks, cleaners, gardeners, or childminders. Economic pressures from the Great Depression took a toll on families, as people moved to find work, delayed marriage and childbearing, and generally struggled. The US government encouraged women to stay home and not work, so as to make it more likely that men (who traditionally earned more money and had more choices of employment) could find jobs. All of these factors led to a reshaped family and altered roles for wives and husbands within them. In the new family, there was greater opportunity for intimacy and companionship between husbands and wives. In the course of the century, positive and affirming depictions of this kind of relationship proliferated, giving rise to our modern, Western conception of marriage as an alliance between two people, built on love, emotional companionship, and sexual intimacy. In many ways, this image of marriage defined, for North America, the twentieth-century values of family, community, and society.

In terms of "This Is Just To Say," I wrote that, given this context, the poem "appears to challenge older ideas about marriage and to embrace new ideas that emphasize shared intimacy, communication, and affectionate companionship. At the same time, the poem makes what we can read as a social phenomenon intensely personal" (p. 65). If we were to phrase this as a research question, we might ask, "How does the depiction of marriage in 'This Is Just To Say' relate to how marriage was understood socially and politically at the time it was written?" Whether we are aiming at proving a thesis statement or answering a research question, we can get there with some hard work, tough thinking, and smooth writing. Let's do it!

****

Katherine Acheson (#084310962)
January 20, 2020

Marriage, Domesticity, and
W. C. Williams's "This Is Just To Say"

"This Is Just To Say" by William Carlos Williams is about the relationship between the speaker or writer of the poem and its listener or reader. Through the choices the poet makes of the form of the poem, its vocabulary, and its grammatical features, we understand that the speaker and the listener are married: their relationship is everyday and down-to-earth; it is between people who have a long and close history together; it is sensual and intimate. The poem depicts what is called "companionate marriage," a term coined in the 1920s to describe "marriage unions held together not by rigid social pressures or religious conceptions of moral duty but by mutual affection, sexual attraction, and equal rights" (Mintz and Kellogg 115). While this form of marriage may appear both natural and normal in our current society, it was (and remains) a historical phenomenon, very much of its time and place,[1] and one which was variously promoted and contested during the period of its ascension. The poem's companion piece, "Reply," written by Williams in the voice of the listener of "This Is Just To Say," expresses a much

---

[1] The emblematic form of companionate marriage joins two people who identify as "opposite" sexes (therefore heteronormative), middle-class and suburban (and therefore white), and procreational; it is a relationship sanctioned and supported by the state and by organized religion.

more perfunctory and traditional view of marriage. In that view, the wife serves the needs of the husband and neither expects nor offers either emotional or sensual intimacy; she does not have equality with him, nor does she seem to seek it. "Reply" contextualizes "This Is Just To Say" and reveals it to be part of a conversation—or perhaps a monologue, given that one person wrote both poems—about marriage in early-twentieth-century America.

"This Is Just To Say" depicts an early-twentieth-century, upper-middle-class American marriage in its material, everyday reality. The choice of words in the poem conveys this. The nouns ("plums," "icebox," and "breakfast," for example) are all concrete things, rather than abstract concepts. "The plums" (l. 2) are specific, physical plums, not metaphors or ideas, and they were in "the icebox" (l. 4), which is also an object with functional properties for the people who own it. "This" in the title is a demonstrative pronoun; it points from the speaker to the poem itself, at least in its own fiction as a note between two people ("this, I.1.a"). "I" and "you" are pronouns whose meaning is relative to who is doing the speaking. As readers of the poem, we infer that "I" and "you" know who each other are, and that there is no ambiguity for them in the communication: the conversation is private to the two of them. These words, the meanings of which we usually take for granted and which we often overlook when we think about the vocabulary of a piece of literature, contribute to the way in which the poem evokes an actual space in which people go about their daily lives and the relationships they have in that space.

The vocabulary of the poem also suggests that sensual and possibly sexual pleasures are routinely shared between the two people. "Plums" are sweet, rich, and velvety; they are also red or purple, both colors associated with the human body and especially with intimate or inner parts ("plum ll.7"). The plums are "delicious," "so sweet," and "so cold"; the experience of eating them is a sensual pleasure. If the language suggests sensuality, the fact that the speaker enjoyed the plums by themself suggests that they denied those pleasures to the reader or listener— pleasures the reader or listener seems to have planned on, as they were "probably/saving [the plums]/for breakfast" (ll. 6-8). The speaker's demand, "Forgive me" (l. 9), can be seen in this context as a slightly dramatic overstatement of transgression and remorse, designed to both acknowledge the sin and deflect or minimize its punishment. The sexual nuances of the description of eating the plums suggests both physical and emotional intimacy between the speaker or writer and the hearer or reader.

The intimacy of "I" to "you" is reinforced by the use of verbs in the poem. The use of the present perfect tense, "I have eaten," which usually describes an action recently completed, initiates a timeline for the poem's events. Within the timeline, we recognize the time immediately before the speaker ate the plums, when the decision was made, and the time immediately after, when they are experienced as "delicious," "so sweet/and so cold" (ll. 10-12). But there is also the future that didn't happen, signaled by the use of the conditional "were probably/saving" (ll. 6-7), in which the recipient of the poem's wishes were fulfilled, and the future that will happen, in which the recipient does—or does not—accede to the demand to "Forgive me" (l. 9). The verbs describe people who live together and have shared history in which their actions impact each other and their preferences and potential reactions are known to each other.

In all these respects—the shared material and everyday reality, the sensual or sexual dimension of the relationship, and the duration and intimacy of the relationship—the poem depicts "companionate marriage." In the ideal of the companionate marriage, wives and husbands share equally in the responsibilities and rewards of marriage; they enjoy each other's love and respect; they freely devote their shared welfare and the sustenance of their nuclear family. With changes in the technology of the home (such as vacuum cleaners and washing machines) that increased the solitude of individuals and couples, especially in an upper-middle-class setting such as that enjoyed by the Williams family and depicted in the poem (Coleman et al. 52), husbands and wives were discovering and experimenting with new ways of communicating and with new forms of intimacy and companionship. In *Images of Family Life in Magazine Advertising, 1920–1978*, Bruce W. Brown says there was a steady rise in the depiction of intimacy between family members (75) and that there was just as steady a decrease in the depiction of wives doing housework (31). While the speaker acknowledges the wife's territorial privileges over the plums, he stresses two other things in their relationship: the enjoyment of shared sensual experience of communicating about experience, about each other's feelings, and about each other's work and life in the household.

When it was published in Williams's *Collected Poems*, "This Is Just to Say" was annotated with a footnote in which readers found another poem, called "Reply." While both poems are by Williams, "Reply" is written in the voice of the recipient of "This Is Just To Say" and is signed "Love. Floss," the familiar name of Williams's wife Florence ("William Carlos Williams"):

"Reply"
(crumped on her desk)

Dear Bill: I've made a
couple of sandwiches for you.
In the ice-box you'll find
blue-berries—a cup of grapefruit
a glass of cold coffee.

On the stove is the tea-pot
with enough tea leaves
for you to make tea if you
prefer—Just light the gas—
boil the water and put it in the tea

Plenty of bread in the bread-box
and butter and eggs—
I didn't know just what to
make for you. Several people
called up about office hours—

See you later. Love. Floss.

Please switch off the telephone.

Like "This Is Just To Say," "Reply" refers to the prosaic, everyday life of a married couple whose long story is made of many short sentences. But unlike "This Is Just To Say," "Reply" resists intimacy, shared history, and the mutual respect of equals. In comparison to the first poem, the view of marriage depicted in "Reply" may strike us as dull and even quietly aggressive, as if the wife is withholding the affection and warmth her husband extends. Floss's resistance to companionate marriage was very much mainstream: in the period, "media portrayals of autonomous women in egalitarian marriages tended to show marriages in trouble until the woman allowed herself to be 'domesticated,' either by having children and settling down or by subordinating herself to the wishes of a strong husband" (Coleman et al. 79).

Complicating matters, however, is the fact that Williams is the author of Floss's voice in this poem. Through that voice he represents a world in which it is women, or rather wives, who reject companionship and affection from their husbands and turn aside from expressions of sensual intimacy and domestic partnership. In the view articulated between the two poems, wives are capable of rejecting what appears, on the surface at least, to be greater equality and respect within marriage, even as their husbands promote those values. However, what appears to be a dialogue in which husband and wife are given equal time is, in fact, a monologue or meditation by Williams on the subjects of his marriage and his wife, and marriage and wives in general. Between the two poems, then, we see how the source or control of representation, or who writes the script for the speaker, powerfully disrupts our ability to read arguments as having "sides," while at the same time ensuring that we understand that one person can entertain many views. "This Is Just To Say" and "Reply" imply that communication is straightforward and unequivocal; together, however, the prove exactly the opposite.

Works Cited (MLA 8 format)

Coleman, Marilyn, et al. *Family Life in 20th-Century America.* Greenwood Press, 2007.

Mintz, Steven, and Susan Kellogg. *Domestic Revolutions: A Social History of American Family Life.* The Free Press, 1988.

"this, pron. and adj." *OED Online*, Oxford UP, December 2019, www.oed.com/view/Entry/200894. Accessed 6 January 2020.

"William Carlos Williams." *Wikipedia: The Free Encyclopedia*, https://en.wikipedia.org/wiki/William_Carlos_Williams. Accessed 10 January 2020.

Williams, William Carlos. "Reply." *The Collected Poems of William Carlos Williams. Volume I: 1909–1939*, edited by A. Walton Litz and Christopher MacGowan, New Directions Press, 1986, p. 536.

——. "This Is Just To Say." *The Collected Poems of William Carlos Williams. Volume I: 1909–1939*, edited by A. Walton Litz and Christopher MacGowan, New Directions Press, 1986, p. 372.

Incorporating Critical Works (Ch. 5)

ASSIGNMENT: Write a six- to eight-page (1,500–2,000 words) essay about "This Is Just To Say" by William Carlos Williams, using the poem, selected critical or theoretical insights collected from scholarly books and journal articles, and any reference works and social or historical contexts you find helpful. The aim of the essay is to help us understand the poem in relation to the full range of resources available, including the critical conversation that is relevant to it. That conversation might be explicitly about the poem, the poet, or his works, or more broadly about some dimension of language, a philosophical concept, a cognitive phenomenon, the characteristics and functions of poetic genres, or any other big question that interests you about the poem, and about which other critical minds have taken an interest.

This kind of essay builds on the work you might do for the other sample essays included in this book. To compose Essay Three, I reviewed the material, including the poetry and my notes from reference works and information about social and historical contexts. I then searched in an online bibliography (*MLAIB*) for various key words and phrases related to "This Is Just To Say," Williams, and the insights I generated in the other two essays. I ended up leafing through (figuratively—I was working online) the tables of contents of all issues of the *William Carlos Williams Review* available to me, which gave me a sense of the kinds of interests scholars have had in WCW's work. Much of the scholarship is about Williams's theories about poetry and those of the groups of poets with whom he was affiliated. Another popular topic is the representation of women across the spectrum of his writing, from journals, to poetics and poems. There is some analysis of Williams's use of genres of poetry, including lyric, of which "This Is Just To Say" is an example.

As we know from my previous essays, I'm interested in language and how poetry produces the illusion of a material world and a conversation within it, and I'm interested in gender and its representation. I'm also interested in poetry in general, and genres of poetry. In addition to sampling essays about Williams and gender, I also read some works about the genre of lyric poetry and his use of the conventions. Jonathan Culler's 2015 book *Theory of the Lyric* provided a rich and interesting survey of the genre from ancient Greek poetry to the present and undergirds some of my analysis. But, as usual, I discovered this essay as I wrote it, re-wrote it, read it, and re-read it. Good luck with yours.

HOW HARD HAS THIS BEEN, PROF A?

I have to admit—well I don't have to, but I'm going to—that writing these sample essays has been hard for me, and they got progressively harder; this last one has been the most difficult.

Critical theory and scholarly interpretations are built over many years, even the length of careers, within contexts that are rich and diverse and that can be sustaining and rewarding, although they are not always. Published literary criticism and theory are serious, complex, demanding things to read and to write; their authors have usually chosen the field or topic, and have worked in it for years. You are not expected, even as an upper-level undergraduate, to be able to work with ease and fluency with these ideas and concepts. In my classes, the priority for me for my students is that they learn to use some of the tools and expertise that already exists in order to open up literature and theory for their own knowledge, enjoyment, and empowerment. I'm happy facilitating that conversation and those discoveries, and I teach a range of subjects.

As a scholar, however, I work on topics that are all set within a particular national and historical context (British literature 1500-1700). I read and write essays and books within the context of a conversation that has been going on for a long time, and which I have been part of for thirty years. The boundaries of it shift and break, but the people in it share some common touchstones and they are expected to acknowledge them. For instance, we don't agree about what Shakespeare's work means, what value it has, or how we should come to conclusions about those things—and we never will. But we have all read much of Shakespeare's work, we know central arguments about that work that have come out in the last 20 years or so, and the historical, linguistic, and social contexts are familiar to us. If we don't know them, we know how to find out about them, and we understand the terms under which they are written. Because of my training and the confines of my career, I don't really know much about Williams or "This Is Just To Say" or the social, historical, and literary contexts of the first half of the twentieth century in the United States. To tell you the truth, it was hard for me to understand what the take-aways are from the articles I read, and I'm not super-confident in the persuasiveness or value of the result.

Does this sound familiar to you? I think it's been a good experience for me—my understanding of what it's like for you, as an undergraduate student, to approach an essay assignment in an upper-level literature course has been enhanced. It's made me think that I need to learn and teach more about how to handle those feelings (of ignorance, or even of intimidation and aversion) in my classrooms. It reminds me of why I started teaching the things in this book—that there is nothing natural about the essay form, and what you already know isn't necessarily helpful. It strengthened my commitment to work with students to identify quality resources and to scaffold their knowledge as they build more and more complex arguments. It has also encouraged me to find diverse ways to reach the learning outcomes in my courses, so that inexperience with or aversion to the essay form doesn't prevent students from learning or me from teaching effectively.

****

English 430
Professor Supercalifragilisticexpialidocious
Katherine Acheson (084310962)
July 8, 2020

Lyric and Sexism in W. C. Williams's "This Is Just To Say"

"This Is Just To Say" by William Carlos Williams is a lyric poem about the relationship between the speaker or writer of the poem and its listener or reader. Through the choices the poet makes of the form of the poem, its vocabulary, and its grammatical features, we understand that the speaker and the listener are married: their relationship is everyday and down-to-earth; it is between people who have a long and close history together; it is sensual and intimate. The poem depicts what is called "companionate marriage," a term coined in the 1920s to describe "marriage unions held together not by rigid social pressures or religious conceptions of moral duty but by mutual affection, sexual attraction, and equal rights" (Mintz and Kellogg 115). The poem's companion piece, "Reply," written by Williams in the voice of Flossie, the recipient of "This Is Just To Say," expresses a much more perfunctory and traditional view of marriage. In that view, the wife serves the needs of the husband and neither expects nor offers either emotional or sensual intimacy; she does not have equality with him, nor does she seem to seek it.

Together the two poems reveal what many critics identify as sexism in Williams's representation of women, and especially of the figure of the wife in his poems about domestic life. However, not all critics agree that Williams's work is sexist. Some temper the claim with evidence that he supported women's rights in social matters, such as the right to vote for qualified white women. Others rationalize Williams's sexism by appealing to the conventions of lyric poetry which prioritize subjective perceptions and experiences. Within that argument, it is the quality and resonance of the expression, and not the ethical or social content, that establish the value of the poem. Criticism of the poem, then, articulates one of the key conflicts in modern literary studies: can we appreciate the craft and beauty of a poem which expresses ideological views that we acknowledge as harmful? Or is aestheticizing sexism just putting lipstick on a pig?

"This Is Just To Say" depicts an early-twentieth-century, upper-middle-class American marriage in its material, everyday, reality. The choice of words in the poem conveys this. The nouns ("plums," "icebox," and "breakfast," for example) are all concrete things, rather than abstract concepts. The vocabulary of the poem also suggests that sensual and possibly sexual pleasures are routinely shared between the two people. "Plums" are sweet, rich, and velvety; they are also red or purple, both colors associated with the human body and especially with intimate or inner parts ("plum II.7"). The plums are "delicious," "so sweet," and "so cold"; the experience of eating them is a sensual pleasure. If the language suggests sensuality, the fact that the speaker enjoyed the plums by themself suggests that they denied those pleasures to the reader or listener—pleasures the reader or listener seems to have planned on, as they were "probably/saving [the plums]/ for breakfast" (ll. 6-8). The sexual nuances of the description of eating the plums suggest both physical and emotional intimacy between the speaker or writer and the hearer or reader. The intimacy of "I" to "you," and the sense of their shared history, is reinforced by the use of verbs in the poem, such as the use of the present perfect tense ("I have eaten"), which usually describes an action recently completed. Within the timeline initiated by this verb, we recognize the moment immediately before the speaker ate the plums when the decision was made to eat them, and the time immediately after, when they are experienced as "delicious," "so sweet/and so cold" (ll. 10-12). But there is also the future that didn't happen, signaled by the use of the conditional "were probably/saving" (ll. 6-7) in which the recipient of the poem's wishes were fulfilled, and the future that will happen, in which the recipient does—or does not—accede to the demand to "Forgive me" (l. 9). The verbs describe people who live together and have shared history in which their actions impact each other and their preferences and potential reactions are known to each other.

In all these respects—the shared material and everyday reality, the sensual or sexual dimension of the relationship, and the duration and intimacy of the relationship—the poem depicts "companionate marriage." In the ideal of the companionate marriage, wives and husbands share equally in the responsibilities and rewards of marriage; they enjoy each other's love and respect; they freely devote their shared welfare and the sustenance of their nuclear family. While the speaker acknowledges the wife's territorial privileges over the plums, he stresses two other things in their relationship: the enjoyment of shared sensual experience of communicating about experience, about each other's feelings, and about each other's work and life in the household.

When it was published in Williams's *Collected Poems*, "This Is Just To Say" was annotated with a footnote in which readers found another poem, called "Reply." While both poems are by Williams, "Reply" is written in the voice of the recipient of "This Is Just To Say" and is signed "Love. Floss," the familiar name of Williams's wife Florence ("William Carlos Williams"):

"Reply"
(crumped on her desk)

Dear Bill: I've made a
couple of sandwiches for you.
In the ice-box you'll find
blue-berries—a cup of grapefruit
a glass of cold coffee.

On the stove is the tea-pot
with enough tea leaves
for you to make tea if you
prefer—Just light the gas—
boil the water and put it in the tea

Plenty of bread in the bread-box
and butter and eggs—
I didn't know just what to
make for you. Several people
called up about office hours—

See you later. Love. Floss.

Please switch off the telephone.

Like "This Is Just To Say," "Reply" refers to the prosaic, everyday life of a married couple whose long story is made of many short sentences. But unlike "This Is Just To Say," "Reply" resists intimacy, shared history, and the mutual respect of equals. In the view articulated between the two poems, wives are capable of rejecting what appears, on the surface at least, to be greater equality and respect within marriage, even as their husbands promote those values. However, both poems are written by Williams: what appears to be a dialogue in which husband and wife are given equal time is, in fact, a monologue or meditation by Williams on the subjects of his marriage and his wife, and marriage and wives in general.

Most critics identify Williams as a sexist writer whose poetry represents him in terms typical of patriarchal discourse about masculinity: "the self-image Williams projects in his writing," writes Graham, is one "of the male artist replete with sexual vigor in pursuit of the generic woman" (166). Celia Carlson writes that "much of Williams's energy in his lyric poetry comes from his attempts to harness what he viewed in rather traditional terms as the feminine power of the body" (Carlson 27). By and large, according to Graham, Williams's writing reflects his conviction that marriage was both what kept him grounded in the present and the material and what prevented him from fulfilling himself as a writer and genius: "How he portrayed his wife and marriage in his writing over fifty years is directly related to that self-image and the dream of merging with this ever-appealing, ever-receptive woman" (Graham 166). Whenever his wife appears, as we see in "Reply," "the writing is not *about* her but about her relation to him" (Graham 170; emphasis in original). "In the drama of their life together, one of the most compelling stories he knew, Williams portrayed himself as the tormented artist, repeatedly tempted to overthrow his conventional life—represented by Flossie—and repeatedly retreating into the familiar and certain still center she provided" (Graham 170). Williams's objectifying description of the female body within stories that are set in medical practice (Schnur) and his frequent representation of unfaithful husbands (Graham 170)—both reflective of his real life—do little to provide relief from the charge that his work is deeply sexist and that he regarded his wife and other women as less than equal to him.

Critics who defend Williams's representation of gender and sex do not typically draw upon evidence of his behavior outside of authorship or offer alternative readings of the representation of gender and sex in his literary work to do so. Rather, they attempt to elevate the literary and philosophical values of the work above its content, its design above its impact, its theoretical finesse above the meaning we might ordinarily take from it. Some critics displace Williams's discourse about female bodies onto theoretical paradigms, especially those espoused or developed by Williams and his peers (Imagist and Modernist poets, for the most part). Celia Carlson, for example, aligns the female body as a form with literature as a formal activity, thereby elevating Williams's objectification of women as itself a literary achievement. Likewise,

Emily Lambeth-Climaco asserts that Williams's treatment of objects, in the context of his much-repeated dictum that there are "No ideas but in things," "signifies reaching after a consummate mode of contact, one that bridges the gulf between individual experience and the real world" (36). Charles Altieri attests to the understanding of the (or his) human condition that the speaker of "This Is Just To Say" attains in the process of the poem: "The justness of the speaker's note is its recognition of his weakness and its lovely combination of self-understanding with an implicit faith in his wife's capacity to understand and accept his deed and, beyond that, to comprehend his human existence as a balance of weakness, self-knowledge, and concern" (501).

For these critics, the form of the lyric itself transcends the dross of earthly inequities and the social burdens of sexual difference. Lyric poetry, according to Jonathan Culler, is a "subjective form" in which "the lyric poet absorbs into himself the external world and stamps it with inner consciousness, and the unity of the poem is provided by this subjectivity" (1). It is subjectivity—the experience of the self—that is the fundamental topic of the lyric poem, and the value of the poem lies in its capacity to convey that subjectivity. The poem is real in ways that its content is not: in "This Is Just To Say," writes Altieri, "we are dealing with two speech acts—one by a character in the poem which is to be assessed dramatically, and one by an implicit poet which invites us to draw parallels between the dramatic situation and general aesthetic considerations" (499-500). The second speech act is the one that constitutes the poem and the one through which the other is framed and our interpretation is conditioned. In these terms, any offensive content or context is not meaningful in terms of our valuation of the poem; it is outside the subjective experience of the poetic consciousness represented therein. The lyric form and the critics who respect its power, beauty, and complexity have the capacity to make sexism, and other social phenomena with which they engage, invisible, or, at least, inscrutable.

Works Cited

Altieri, Charles. "Presence and Reference in a Literary Text: The Example of Williams' 'This Is Just To Say.'" *Critical Inquiry*, vol. 5, no. 3, 1979, pp. 489-510.

Ashton, Jennifer. "Lyric, Gender, and Subjectivity in Modern and Contemporary Women's Poetry." *The Cambridge History of American Women's Literature*, Cambridge UP, 2012, pp. 515-38.

Carlson, Celia. "Compelling Objects: Form and Emotion in Williams's Lyric Poetry." *William Carlos Williams Review*, vol. 26, no. 1, 2006, pp. 27-50.

Culler, Jonathan. *Theory of the Lyric*. Harvard UP, 2015. E-book version.

Graham, Theodora R. "Williams, Flossie, and the Others: The Aesthetics of Sexuality." *Contemporary Literature*, vol. 28, no. 2, 1987, pp. 163-86.

Hilldebrandt, Claudia, et al. "Theories of Lyric." *Journal of Literary Theory*, vol. 11, no. 1, 2017, pp. 1-11.

Lambeth-Climaco, Emily. "'This Rhetoric is Real': William Carlos Williams's Recalibration of Language and Things." *William Carlos William Review*, vol. 28, nos. 1-2, 2008, pp. 35-53.

Mintz, Steven, and Susan Kellogg. *Domestic Revolutions: A Social History of American Family Life*. The Free Press, 1988.

Morris, Daniel. "This Is Just To Say This Is the End of Art: Williams and the Aesthetic Attitude." *William Carlos William Review*, vol. 32, nos. 1-2, 2015, pp. 53-65.

"plum, n. and adj.2." *OED Online*, Oxford UP, December 2019, www.oed.com/view/Entry/146028. Accessed 6 January 2020.

Schnur, Kate. "'I found another to admire': The Thing of the Female Body in William Carlos Williams's Medical Narratives." *William Carlos Williams Review*, vol. 33, nos. 1-2, 2016, pp. 172-88.

"William Carlos Williams." *Wikipedia: The Free Encyclopedia*, https://en.wikipedia.org/wiki/William_Carlos_Williams. Accessed 10 January 2020.

Williams, William Carlos. "Reply." *The Collected Poems of William Carlos Williams. Volume I: 1909–1939*, edited by A. Walton Litz and Christopher MacGowan, New Directions Press, 1986, p. 536.

——. "This Is Just To Say." *The Collected Poems of William Carlos Williams. Volume I: 1909–1939*, edited by A. Walton Litz and Christopher MacGowan, New Directions Press, 1986, p. 372.

Works Cited

Altieri, Charles. "Presence and Reference in a Literary Text: The Example of Williams' 'This Is Just to Say.'" *Critical Inquiry*, vol. 5, no. 3, 1979, pp. 489–510.

Brown, Bruce W. *Images of Family Life in Magazine Advertising, 1920–1978*. Praeger, 1981.

Carlson, Allan. *The "American Way": Family and Community in the Shaping of the American Identity*. ISI Books, 2003.

Carlson, Celia. "Compelling Objects: Form and Emotion in Williams's Lyric Poetry." *William Carlos Williams Review*, vol. 26, no. 1, 2006, pp. 27–49.

The Chicago Manual of Style. 15th ed., U of Chicago P, 2003.

Coleman, Marilyn, et al. *Family Life in 20th-Century America*. Greenwood, 2007.

Davis, Simone Weil. *Living up to the Ads: Gender Fictions of the 1920s*. Duke UP, 2000.

Graham, Theodora R. "Williams, Flossie, and the Others: The Aesthetics of Sexuality." *Contemporary Literature*, vol. 28, no. 2, 1987, pp. 163–86.

Imlah, Mick. "Imagism." *The Oxford Companion to Twentieth-Century Poetry in English*, edited by Ian Hamilton, Oxford UP, 1996.

The Johns Hopkins Guide to Literary Theory and Criticism. Edited by Michael Groden, Martin Kreiswirth, and Imre Szeman, Johns Hopkins UP, 2005, http://litguide.press.jhu.edu/.

Johnson, Bob. "'A Whole Synthesis of His Time': Political Ideology and Cultural Politics in the Writings of William Carlos Williams, 1929–1939." *American Quarterly*, vol. 54, no. 2, 2002, pp. 179–215.

The Milton Reading Room. Edited by Thomas Luxon, Dartmouth College, 1997–2010, http://www.dartmouth.edu/~milton/reading_room/contents/index.shtml.

MLA International Bibliography. Modern Language Association, 2020, https://www.mla.org/Publications/MLA-International-Bibliography.

Modern Language Association of America. *MLA Handbook*. 8th ed., Modern Language Association, 2016.

Morris, Daniel. "The Erotics of Close Reading: Williams, Demuth, and 'The Crimson of Cyclamen.'" *William Carlos Williams Review*, vol. 27, no. 1, 2007, pp. 57–68.

The Oxford Companion to Twentieth-Century Poetry in English. Edited by Ian Hamilton. Oxford UP, 1996.

Oxford Reference Online, http://www.oxfordreference.com. Accessed 3 October 2009.

Shakespeare, William. "Sonnet 130." *The Norton Shakespeare*, edited by Stephen Greenblatt et al., 2nd ed., W.W. Norton, 2008, p. 1798.

Tufte, Edward. *The Cognitive Style of PowerPoint™: Pitching Out Corrupts Within*. 2nd ed., Graphics Press, 2006.

"William Carlos Williams." *Wikipedia, The Free Encyclopedia*. Wikimedia Foundation, 17 June 2010, http://en.wikipedia.org/wiki/William_Carlos_Williams. Accessed 5 July 2010.

Williams, William Carlos. *Autobiography*. Random House, 1951.

——. *The Collected Poems of William Carlos Williams, 1909–1939*. Edited by A. Walton Litz and Christopher MacGowan, vol. 1, New Directions, 1986.

——. *Paterson*. Edited by Christopher MacGowan, rev. ed., New Directions, 1992.

——. *Selected Essays*. New Directions, 1954.

——. *The William Carlos Williams Reader*. Edited by M.L. Rosenthal. J. Laughlin for New Directions, 1966.

Wimsatt, W.K., and Monroe Beardsley. "The Intentional Fallacy." *The Verbal Icon: Studies in the Meaning of Poetry*, UP of Kentucky, 1954, pp. 3–18.

Permissions
Acknowledgment

Subject Index

From the Publisher

A NAME NEVER SAYS IT ALL, BUT THE WORD "BROADVIEW" expresses a good deal of the philosophy behind our company. We are open to a broad range of academic approaches and political viewpoints. We pay attention to the broad impact book publishing and book printing has in the wider world; for some years now we have used 100% recycled paper for most titles. Our publishing program is internationally oriented and broad-ranging. Our individual titles often appeal to a broad readership too; many are of interest as much to general readers as to academics and students.

Founded in 1985, Broadview remains a fully independent company owned by its shareholders—not an imprint or subsidiary of a larger multinational.

For the most accurate information on our books (including information on pricing, editions, and formats) please visit our website at www.broadviewpress.com. Our print books and ebooks are also available for sale on our site.

broadview press
www.broadviewpress.com

MIX
Paper from
responsible sources
FSC® C013916